LESSONS THROUGH REFLECTIONS:

CHANGING THE WORLD IN A NEW DIRECTION

JAY SOOKNANAN

NEWMAN SPRINGS PUBLISHING
320 Broad Street
Red Bank, NJ 07701

First originally published by Newman Springs Publishing 2021

ISBN 978-1-63881-464-1 (Paperback)
ISBN 978-1-63881-465-8 (Digital)

Printed in the United States of America

To my future children and future generations to come.

*To my family, my friends, my team, and all
the positive influences in my life.*

*We change the world one person at a time,
and the first person to start with is the person in the mirror.*

CONTENTS

PREFACE

What is the purpose of this book?

To reflect on my life and show real-life issues and ways we can move on to make a better place for future generations and explore what we can implement to heal the world.

Descriptive, fun, dramatic, relatable, relative, and relevant.

To show why things happen, the conversation around nature versus nurture, and how we can raise our kids differently.

Hitting all major topics: healing the planet, religion, violence, sex, drugs, cops.

I want to cast a vision for the future and produce something inspirational and motivational while sharing life-coaching lessons for success and life principles.

I aim to produce something vulnerable, fun, exciting, and connecting. I want to share stories behind why I made certain life choices and offer some cautionary tales.

How do I know this will happen?

You are the author of your life. You are the reason you are where you are. Yes, sure, we all come from different circumstances. The past is already written, but the future is up to you. You have to know and remind yourself that you matter. You are worth it.

I was inspired by a video on Facebook of a thirteen-year-old girl imploring the government to protect the environment. She was speaking up on this cause at such a young age. If we cannot fix the planet, at least don't destroy it. It is about the future generations. You say you care; let your actions prove it. We can help. She is young and has less opportunity—"the girl who silenced the world for five minutes."

INTRODUCTION

I woke up, opened my eyes, and looked to the left of me, seeing my beautiful lady rolled up in the blanket, sleeping on her side and I leaned over and kissed her on the forehead.

I looked down at my body. I have abs, a sculpted chest, and a beautiful body. I'm looking at myself in the bed. I was pleased with my physique, like I was waking up out of a dream.

I couldn't believe where I was. I got up, and I walked over to my window and felt the bliss and sense of accomplishment as I saw my beautiful patio, the sun shining through the glass. I was in my boxers. I placed my hands on my waist, and I allowed the sun to shine on me as if God was showering me with his blessings. I smiled, and happy thoughts rushed my mind.

I put my trunks on and went downstairs through our balcony and personal patio, down to the pool.

I did twenty laps to wake up and returned upstairs. When my girl came out of the bedroom with her robe, the maid had already set up breakfast on the patio.

She saw me.

I was using my towel to dry myself and to shake my hair.

As she watched me, her face said, "Damn, that's my man." I continued to walk over, gave her another kiss on her forehead, wrapped the towel around my waist, and sat down at the table.

Our mothers joined us. We enjoyed breakfast and had a good time talking and laughing about the night we just had.

After breakfast was done, I went downstairs through the house to pray, practice positive affirmations, reminiscing on our beautiful breakfast. The fruits—their freshness—reminded me of the purity of our life.

Feeling serene and blissful, I went down to our in-home gym to work out a little bit and get in some weight training and calisthenics. Veni joined me. We did a few ab exercises together. Then she did her thing while I went into the sauna to relax and have another moment of peace and gratitude.

While meditating, I focused on all the things that I have to be grateful for and worked on my chanting. I am thankful for my beautiful mansion, the amazing gym, our beautiful sauna, my beautiful wife, my family, my team, my friends, the universe, my vision, my purpose, and the bliss.

I got up, showered, and got dressed in a nice, relaxed state, just moving with such ease.

Time wasn't flying by.

It was moving at my pace.

I went upstairs back to the patio. Everything was cleaned. There was a beverage waiting for me, and my laptop was set up. I was about to get on a conference with the board members of the world peace project.

Ring, ring, ring.

BOOM

Boom, I woke up.

My mom was slapping me in my head with a cellphone.

It was twenty years earlier.

Then I was a rebellious teenager. I was fourteen or fifteen.

I hung out all night. I was getting drunk and high. I didn't care about anything. Every response was "I do not care" and "I know."

I slept in the living room on a couch. My mom was fed up. As she was hitting me, I laughed. That's why she picked up the phone to strike me. That made me laugh even more while hiding under the covers.

It's a really blissful time.

Well, not really blissful. Kind of painful but funny. To me, anyway.

Later that night, I sat up with my sister. Before we ate, we reflected on the day, and as I watched her and watched myself, I started reminiscing about how everything—my whole life—started.

As I was born, my father was heading down the wrong path. After his mom passed when he was sixteen, he stopped caring about life. He started fighting, getting into trouble, and living life on the edge, without fear or regard for others.

Even before his mom passed, he always had an entrepreneur kind of lifestyle. He learned to make an honest living from selling produce in the market with his mom, and then his father took his mom's money and gambled with it. His father did manage to buy a house and more through gambling. My father learned how to sell and smoke weed from his other associations as well.

Your parents affect the way your mind develops. My father learned the value of hard work and how to sell goods and negotiate from working with his mom. From his dad, he learned to take risks.

Like his father, he had a temper as well. One time, my mom was working in the market for him, and this lady working there threw a bucket of water at her. My mom told my dad. My dad overreacted and threw a two-pound weight at the lady's head and missed. Then he threw a one-pound weight, splitting her head open. That young lady threw water on Mommy because she liked my father, but that lady was the sister of one of the biggest gunmen in Trinidad. My father had to leave and actually hid right in the gunman's family house. He left as soon as he could.

He came up to America, and my mom came up right after him. He worked for an Italian couple, and the husband, Sal, really liked my father and helped him and mommy with their papers.

My father went down some crazy paths. He acquired a storefront, a garage where he worked on cars, and a house on Pennsylvania Avenue. That came from him working hard, mainly. He worked painting buses, and one day he ended up hijacking a gas station.

It was all planned out. It was supposed to be easy. One of the guys in on the heist was supposed to be working at the gas station that night, but he ended up calling out of work. Guess he chickened out.

The other guy there with my pops wanted to back out, and my father said, "No, we're going to go through with it."

Even though everybody else wanted to back off, he went ahead. He walked up with the shotgun by the side of his leg. He walked up to this massive black cashier, kicked the gun up, and cocked it back.

He said he took the money and started his new life. When the changes started happening, he went further down the wrong path and started drugs. He always smoked weed, but now he started doing crack and coke, hanging out with the wrong people, cheating on my mom, and doing a whole bunch of crazy and dangerous things.

One time, my brother told me my father put a gun in his diaper. The cops were approaching the car, and my father needed to hide the gun.

My big brother, my sister, and my mom faced the brunt of my father's craziness.

My mom was a strong woman, from what I experienced. She was hardworking and made things happen.

She had his back, so he could have become whatever he wanted. He just made the wrong decisions, got into crack, and destroyed all his assets, his income, his shop, his garage, his home, and his family.

What comes quickly withers just as fast.

Going through the fast life and not working legitimately, you build a poor foundation. Usually cutting corners and not having the best practices or legal practices, you know where you will end up; it is only a matter of time. If you want wealth, it has to be built on an honest foundation, with good morals and ethics, for it to last and be strong.

I was born on May 12, Mother's Day. On that day, my mom thought I was special to be born on Mother's Day, but the nurse said, "Do you think you're special? You are due tomorrow."

My mom knew she would have me on Mother's Day but didn't say anything.

Am I supposed to be special? Are we not all special?

In the beginning, my mom didn't even want to feed me. She was so hurt; she was going through postpartum depression from what was going on in her life. My father was to the point where he would even take the EBT card for drugs.

They faced a lot of struggles, from all the stories I heard and the experiences I had.

My life started at the end of something good, gone bad.

New beginnings, starting back at rock bottom. Was I a problem child or a gift?

I came, and wow, what a life to come into.

I was full of joy, but my mom was in depression. She was stuck. She didn't want to feed me, and they were about to send her to the crazy house because of it. My grandma came up to Brooklyn and took my brother, my sister, my mom, and me back home to Trinidad. My mom was able to catch and heal herself and come out of that depressed state. She started working with my aunt; they opened up a store. Mom worked in the store.

My family from back home was very well-off. My great grandfather was an amazing man.

He owned a lumberyard. He bought a lot of real estate and set up each of his grandchildren with homes. My mom, her siblings, and all her cousins had houses. His family was set up from one man.

One man can make a difference for generations to come.

My mom rehabilitated herself, and when I was two and a half years old, she came back up here to New York with my brother and sister to create a life for us. She left me in Trinidad.

I was back in Trini, where we had everything. We lived in a nice house with a coconut tree, video games (Atari), and all the new gadgets. We even had the Batman and Flintstones cars. I used to run around barefoot, smiling. My grandma rocked me on the rocking chair, holding me close to her chest, while she pushed my cousin on the hammock. Before my auntie Nadia went out with her boyfriend Hameraj, who is now her husband, she would sing me to sleep and read me my prayers.

Many people poured love into me. Everybody poured their blessings into me. Thank you, God.

Then at four and a half, I came up to America.

I saw things I had never seen before. In Trinidad, all I knew was homes and big houses. Then I came up here, and I saw an apartment for the first time. I was happy to see my beautiful mom and my siblings; nothing else really mattered.

I guess that feeling has made me a family man. I saw the value of a village earlier in life because I did not have my immediate family in my life the whole time. My village is an amazing support system. You do not know what you have until it is not there.

Even at a young age, I could sense that my mom was struggling. I never wanted to ask for anything. She gave us everything we needed, she treated us like kings and queens, and she didn't make us do much work. She really didn't make us do any work. I didn't want to be a burden on her, so if I could cook for myself, I would.

Anything I could do on my own, I did it. Though I never really asked for too much help, my family was always there for me.

I had my siblings. My big sister really had my back, but I didn't want to burden anybody.

When I went to school, I was very charismatic. I would walk down the block and just say "Hi" to everybody. I would walk into the mechanic shop, open the door, and say, "Hey, how are you doing?" I would walk into the Anchor, where the brokers worked, and say, "Hey, good morning, guys."

We sold them candy and stuff like that to fund school trips and win awards. I remember winning a blow-up beanbag one time. I knew many people well at five years old. That was my attitude, walking to school, being charismatic.

"Hey, how you doing? Good morning. Good morning."

As a young kid, we are full of joy and openness because we are grateful and content. As we grow older, we realize all the things we do not have and want more, without realizing how much we have.

When you are grateful, you treat the things you own better. When you count your blessings, you have more blessings to count, allowing you to work for more.

The thing is, you cannot really have much more without working with others, and there are more people we do not know than people we do know. The world even conditions us not to trust others, such as not talking to strangers. Leadership expert John Maxwell says, if you work by yourself, you will always be small potatoes, nothing wrong with small potatoes, but they just do not last long. If you have big dreams, you have to work with others. We are being conditioned for lack and fear.

I'm not saying not to be cautious but have faith. Network and grow.

I went to school, and I had a really good experience there. I met my best friend, Sam. We kicked it off since kindergarten, actually since we met in pre-K. I actually didn't end up going to pre-K after the first few days because no one could drop me off to school and pick me up. I played a lot of *Super Mario Bros.* and Nintendo that year.

Later, when I was five years old and in kindergarten, I remember this lady, Maria, the attendance lady, held my hand. She asked me, "What do you want to be when you grow up?"

I said, "A doctor."

She said, "You'll be a doctor," and looked into my eyes, giving me conviction. She gave me the confidence, the belief. Sometimes, people believe in you before you believe in yourself, and you live through their conviction as your own belief builds.

I wanted to become a cardiologist because my mom's boyfriend was hospitalized with a heart issue. I liked him, even though he wasn't my father. I pushed him away. I didn't want to listen to him. He was really a good guy, and I didn't like to see him hurt. I didn't even know what pain looked like until that time. I never saw anyone hurt and in a hospital.

Your childhood and coping methods help mold your decision about what you want to be.

I feel that's what made me decide to want to be a cardiologist. When I was seven years old, my uncle Imrit and my mom had my little sister. Uncle is what we called my mom's boyfriend; we say it out of respect for our elders.

I didn't like for my mom to be working so hard, especially with this new child coming. I saw she was already working too hard. So I started doing laundry for the whole family. I tried to do the dishes and make my brother's food as often as I could, so my mom wouldn't have to do it. His sandwiches and things. My family treated my brother really well, and my big sister even took care of us at one point.

My sister really nurtured us; she was like a mother to us as well. She helped me with my studies and taught me a lot of good things.

Once, I was taking the whole family's laundry, which was bigger than me. I fell over the curb because I couldn't see it. I learned to look at the side of the cart and bend it back above the curb.

I learned to work hard, well harder than the average seven-year-old. Before my aunt passed away around Christmas 2018, I went to visit her a lot. She told me, "You know, when you were seven years old, you were a wicked little boy?"

I asked her, "What do you mean, wicked?"

She was like, "Yeah, you would come into the store, asking me for a job."

I couldn't believe it. Well, I guess I was counting my mom's money. She made ends meet, but I didn't know if she was under or over $10 on her balance.

She gave us everything. She gave us her all.

That's why since I was young, I have wanted to give her a better life. I want to be able to help her because she gave everything, with a smile on her face.

I was a troublesome kid at one point. I grew up with an Italian family, which was what our neighborhood was primarily composed of. My brother is nine years older than me. We watched *Analyze This*, a movie with a predominately Italian cast, and I became a professional curser. I was five or six.

I became one of the best cursers. I used to even curse my own mom.

I loved her so much, yet I used to get aggravated for no reason. Maybe I was frustrated about not being able to spend enough time with her, or maybe it was her trying to be a parent. I don't know. I can't remember.

Growing up, I would go to Trinidad every summer. I enjoyed those summers, really connecting with my cousins as well. We had a great time, getting lots of family time and making a lot of connections. We had a good life growing up.

I did well in school and got the most awards, the top grades in my classes, a full four in my math and a three in my reading. They put me in the superintendent's program for advanced students in sixth grade. Since I was young, the universe was kind of nurturing me to be a lawyer, with lots of little whispers. I guess because of my way with words and love of arguing. I feel this way because when I went to the sixth grade, they put me into a law class.

I fought being a lawyer because I always heard lawyers were liars. I did not like to lie.

I continued on that path to becoming a doctor and did really well in school. I would always be the first kid there to help the teacher set up the room. I used to get up at 5:00 or 5:30 a.m. before anybody else in the house, especially before my brother had to go to work because I didn't want anybody to stop me from going to the bathroom. I wanted to be early to school, but I would still make breakfast for my little sister.

Even in elementary school, I dropped my little sister off to school before I went to school.

I was always one of the hardest workers I knew.

I tried to work as hard as I could, but I didn't compare myself to anybody else. I just tried to do as much as I could do for the people around me and serve them to the highest level.

In sixth grade, I did really well again, making friends with an eighth-grader so that no one would ever bully me.

It was about making connections with the right people.

This time, I went to school all by myself. All my friends were gone because I had moved on to a different school for a better education.

Right away, I made a name for myself. I had this charisma, this energy that made me popular among my classmates. Looking back on my life, I was always a leader. I had many people willing to listen to me; they backed me up because I had a good heart. I cared about people. I got it from my mama. I wanted to be my best.

Respect is earned; it is given when you work to the best of your ability.

One day, my brother and I got into a fight. I was home, and I was playing a fighting video game, *Def Jam*.

He had work in the morning. He was tired and was like, "Jay, shut up. I got to go to sleep. Stop making so much noise."

I lowered the volume all the way down, but to win a video game, you have to smash the buttons. I didn't know he was getting irritated. The lights were off, and the room was dark. He picked me up, and he threw me into the windowsill.

We slept on the same bed together. He may have meant to throw me on the bed, but he launched me into the windowsill and busted my head open. I didn't realize it yet; the lights were off. I didn't know I was bleeding or anything. I cried for about five to ten seconds, then my mom said, "Shut up and go to sleep."

So I shut up, and I went to sleep. I woke up the next day and saw what had happened to me.

No one did anything, not my mom or my sister. Only my aunt went to get Neosporin and put it on my head.

Growing up, my brother and sister used to tell me I was the adopted child. They used to try to scare me with ghost stories when Mommy was out for the night. They would leave me in the room by myself and bang the doors and walls, saying, "Hello? Is that you?" trying to act like there was a ghost in the house.

We had a lot of fun. We played hide-and-seek and the three blind mice.

My brother is nine years older than I am. He and his friends would do wicked stuff to me. He tried to make me smack myself in the face with shaving cream and other stupid things. Whatever, I wasn't scared, though. I was the kind of dude that would pick up a knife and chase him around the house. I was wild. I had fun. I would take on any challenge.

With my big sister, we had these moments where we would sit on this big inflatable Arizona can and use the open oven door as our table. We would put our glasses and our food on it. We loved bologna sandwiches.

People complained about bologna being a meal, but we loved it. We were good friends; we would eat our food together and have a lot of good times. She loved to listen to love songs and to watch TV every night.

She did her homework late at night, using the light shining in through the window from the streetlight to see. She was scared Mommy would beat her if Mommy knew she didn't do her homework but said she did.

Procrastination was a habit. It led her all through college and gave her a lot of stress.

After that fight with my brother, I didn't like him too much. Now, I'm the godfather of his daughter, and we have a good relationship. But at that point, I hated him.

I was a fighter as well. In second grade, I beat up a kid because he wouldn't stop talking to a girl who asked me to tell him to stop.

He did not want to stop. I asked politely, and I gave him fair warning that if he did not listen, I would hit him.

He did not listen, so I punched him right in the head, grabbed his head, and threw him into the brick wall. I did it as lightly as I could to just shake him up. He kept coming, so I threw him on the table, punched him in the head, and spat on him. I did not want this to happen. I apologized, and the next week, I was having dinner at his house.

Another time, I cursed this kid and said something sexual about his mom. He talked about my mom, and I smacked him so hard across his face, you could see my handprint on his face. He told a teacher, and once I told her what he said about my mom, the lady said, "You want to smack him again?"

I cursed and beat up many kids, even in sixth grade.

I had a few fights there and even almost got suspended. I fought kids double my size; it was not like I was picking on the puny kid. I threw a French fry at this kid, and he threw one covered with ketchup at me. It did not hit me, but I got up and punched him in his nose. He started bleeding. I was sent to the dean's room. I apologized, and that prevented my suspension. I was respectful and was a great student. They never expected me to do anything wrong. I always spoke my way out of trouble.

How you speak and handle situations matters. I spoke up, focused on the key facts, and was apologetic and sincere.

Respect takes you a long way.

My profile as well didn't fit; it was hard to associate good grades and good manners with these behaviors.

The lesson in all of that for me was not to judge a book by its cover.

I learned these habits from the different movies my brother watched as I grew up. I thought acting like that was cool. I did not understand that these actions were really wrong.

Be careful of the media you feed your kids, and if they are exposed to harmful things, explain to them the differences between right and wrong and the consequences of their choices.

When I went to Trinidad that summer, I ended up going to stay with my aunt and grandma, the ones who used to watch me when I was a kid. I asked them, "Do you love me?"

They both said, "Yeah," their faces showing dismay at the question.

I asked, "Can I stay here?" Both said yeah. They convinced me to stay there, and I convinced myself to stay as well.

I was there with my little sister that summer. I loved her so much. We were best friends. She would give me one hundred kisses before we went to sleep. I remember when she was going on the airplane to return to the United States while I was staying back in Trinidad. She looked back at me, and she looked so sad. That was probably one of my first regrets in life. I don't really regret it anymore, but that was my first regret. It still takes my breath when I think about it. Sometimes you need guidance from your parents; I did not know how these actions would affect me.

A lot of things happened that year I stayed in Trinidad. Other kids made fun of me a lot because I was chubby, had a girly voice, and was American. I went to an all-boys school, and I couldn't even go through puberty in peace because I didn't have any privacy. I slept at my grandma's. Kids bullied me; even my own cousins made fun of me because of my weight.

So I didn't want to play cricket with them. One of my cousins continued to make fun of me. When I asked him to stop, he did not stop, so I punched him in his stomach, making him cry and fall on the floor. I was not even upset about it either. I felt it was really wrong for him to keep doing that to me.

My aunt Nadia and her boyfriend, Hameraj, acquired land, and my aunt Shereda started farming on it. Instead of playing cricket, I learned how to farm. I helped her more than any of her kids, and then when I came home, my aunt wanted me to wash the dishes and do more housework as well, while her kids barely did anything. Maybe it was my perception. I was not scared to work; it was better than doing nothing. So I did whatever they needed.

I was always active. I learned about working hard that year. I would even get up at five every morning before any other kids or family. Just my grandma and me. I would water the plants, even wipe the leaves some days, sweep and mop the gallery, and go get the bread, all before anybody else got up.

I would run to the store barefoot, happily. I didn't care that I had to work hard. I was young and innocent and full of energy.

While people were playing, I was working. I learned to enjoy the work and how to work even harder. I even learned how to create routines to stay up on all my activities. I have been training to be a leader since a young kid.

I came back up to America in the eighth grade, my uncle brought me back.

I think he got arrested that time or the time after for smuggling kids up from Trinidad. He had brought a kid up when he brought me.

The only reason he got into trouble was because of the strict immigration laws. It was not like these people were bad. He got deported for it.

Now it's very hard for him to get his papers to come back into the country.

A few extra dollars are not worth the risk sometimes. He could have come up and bought and sold clothes and made more money.

I came back to America, and according to my little sister, I was annoying. Maybe I did pick up annoying tendencies from hanging out with my cousins and became childish. I was more focused and work-oriented when I originally left because I was working to help my family and do well in school. Since then, our relationship has never been the same.

When you work hard, you don't have time for nonsense and wasting energy.

I remember walking to the store with my brother and him buying a case of beer, for whatever they were doing.

I realized at that moment how many opportunities we had here compared to in Trinidad.

I decided I was never going back there to live. I didn't go back for ten years. I stayed as far away as I could. I had missed my mom. I remember crying in the bathroom when I was down there.

Absence makes the heart grow fonder. You do not realize all you have until it is not there.

BECOMING CASUAL

I learned to just go through life, and I became very casual, letting opportunities pass me by. The superintendent wanted me to participate in their program and do two years of schooling at the same time.

I said, "No, I'm okay."

I ended up going to Dyker Heights. I went back and hung out with my old friends, Jack, Peter, and Sam. We had just made friends with Biggs. I went back to my comfort zone.

Stay out of your comfort zone. The growth is on the other side.

Sam and I walked home from school alone. Everyone we knew had people that would pick them up from school, but we didn't. We would walk home from school in the cold or heat.

I would say that no one loves us because no one would pick us up or drop us off to school, except Jack's grandpa every so often.

How do you spell *love*? T-I-M-E, right?

Our families had to work, though. I didn't understand that. I felt unloved.

Eighth grade wrapped up well. I was a chubby kid. I got into one fight. Well, not really. I told this kid he smelled because he would provoke me, but he really did smell.

On my birthday, he came to try and fight me.

He came down by himself, and I was with two big dudes. I said, "Yo, bro, I don't want to fight."

He didn't want to listen. Then a whole group of kids came behind him. It was a bunch of black kids. Then some white kids joined him as well. My friend Sam knew one of the white kids, and he said to one of them, "Hey, you know my cousin, right? Get on this side."

We were about even, and this other black kid came off the side, saying "Let me test this dude," and slapped me in my face. Before his hand could leave my face, my hand took him and threw him to the floor. It was a reaction. I didn't want to fight. I was smiling.

Don't take people's kindness for weakness. You might get smacked in the face.

What could I say? God bless me. I had no fear in my heart. No one fought that day.

That was my biggest memory in eighth grade.

Since I was young, I had a joyful life, even at my fifth-grade prom. Sam and I were known as party animals by our principal.

I received the highest grades as well. It was a foreshadowing. I was a party animal, but I would do very well academically.

Work hard, play hard. Remember to do the work first so you deserve the playtime.

Then I went to ninth grade. That's when the casualness really started affecting me.

BECOMING A CASUALTY

When ninth grade came around, all my friends and I went to New Utrecht High School. It was the closest school around, and we enjoyed ourselves. We started off the year strong, going hard.

When the second semester came around, my friend Sam and I, best friends since we were four or five years old, decided to cut class.

I guess my casualness caught up with me. A lot of kids—the cool kids—were cutting the last two periods of school. I asked him, "Hey, you want to cut the last two periods?"

He said, "Sure."

We ended up going back to my house to my brother's room.

What a journey that led to.

We went to my brother's room to play video games. While we were playing, I saw an envelope with my father's name on it. I hadn't seen my father in about six years since I was eight. I knew him between the ages of five and eight years old.

He stopped talking to us when he asked my mom for all of our social security numbers, insisting he said he could get eighty grand with them.

I didn't trust him. I told my mom not to give it to him.

I saw that package with his name on it. When I looked inside, there was marijuana.

Curiosity may not always kill the cat, but it could make him do some crazy things.

I knew about weed, but I didn't know what to do with it.

We didn't know how to roll it up or anything. I had an idea. "Hey, your brother smokes, right? Let's see if he will roll this up for us."

We went and met with his brother. He rolled it up for us, and we went to smoke down the block with him.

The first time we ever smoked, Sam and I saw it coming, but his brother acted like nothing would happen. We saw cops drive off when we got there, and we went on the stoop and started smoking.

I was sitting on the stoop and was the only one that could see the cars coming up the block.

We were almost done smoking. We didn't get high because we didn't know how to smoke. We were spitting all over the stoop. It was so nasty to us. We did not know how to inhale.

The cops were coming down the block. The lights were off, no sirens, and they were driving slow, right toward us. I said, "Lui, the cops are coming."

He was like, "Jay, don't mess around."

"They are coming. They are right there. Why would I mess around?"

He put it under the mat. The mat luckily had bristles under it. So when he scratched it with the mat, it disappeared.

The cops came, and they checked all of our pockets. Lui was nineteen, and we were both fifteen. We all said we were fifteen because Lui had a baby face, and he had shaved, thank God.

The cops went into my friend's pockets and they pulled out what looked like a Dutch Masters cigar, but it wasn't a Dutch. It was a cigar cologne. I said, "No. It's just cologne." They let us walk away. They thought we were just sitting on someone's stoop. A few moments later, they realized we were smoking weed, and they called us back.

We were walking away, looking at each other, thinking of running. You could see it in our faces. The cops were fat, and we had a good ten yards on them, plus Sam lived right around the block. We ended up turning back around, and they made us scrub up all the spit with newspaper.

That was the first time we ever got high. We got higher from the scare than the weed.

We started smoking regularly after that, especially me. Lui didn't want to hang out with his brother, but he would want to hang out with me. He got me high almost every day, off of high-grade weed. We went down this path, and eventually, all my friends started smoking weed.

I led them down the wrong path.

Ever since I was young, whatever I did influence everyone around me, the whole community. I was able to affect everybody that was associated with us and even people not directly associated with us.

Whatever you do spreads. I guess that is the law of attraction.

Energy travels. It is a frequency and a vibration, so it literally continues to travel.

The second or third time I smoked, I came home, and my eyes were red because I was high.

My mom said, "Oh, you want to be like your father? Why don't you go by him?"

She didn't even try to talk to me or discuss anything.

Remember that you were once young, relate to explain, and guide.

I hadn't seen the guy in six years, but I remembered his phone number. I was at my friend's house one day, and I called him. He said to come. I went over there that day and rolled the biggest Bombaclat—the fattest joint—I ever rolled in my life. I never knew how to roll joints before, only Dutches.

CLASSIFIED AS BAD

From there, a lot changed. Change is constant.

I started being classified as "bad," even though I would do well in school. When people call you bad, you tend to become what people believe about you. That is why it is very important to consider who you let speak things into your life. If people label you bad, you can become bad, especially if it's someone who loves you or someone you care about or have a high regard for. It's kind of what I teach about bullying in schools. Don't call a person a bully. The action he is doing is bullying, but if you call him a bully, you are classifying him, judging him. You are not allowing him to change, and that's what we do in society. Once someone does something we do not agree with, like curse, do drugs, rob, steal, or do things that are not good actions, we call them bad and write them off.

Sometimes, good people make bad decisions, and bad people make good decisions.

With the decisions we make, we have to realize things could go either way. The decisions we make dictate where we go in life, but remember the impact of and difference between nature versus nurture as well. People, society, and institutions are already nurturing us in this life. Nature, our environment, and circumstances are all around us—all those factors play a factor as well.

Everything has good and bad, and we should recognize all sides of people. Again, when our family and our friends are calling us these names, society is calling us these names, and schools are calling us them as well. We can tend to go in that direction, believing that is who we are.

So I started doing bad things. I started to hang out with my father every day possible. I didn't see the things he was doing as bad. I didn't realize they were bad. In my head, I didn't even realize teachers and people in my community were classifying me as bad, and that was why I was doing these actions. That is what was happening, subconsciously. I was classified.

I started hanging out with my father, living with him for about two years. I learned how to bag up weed and, every now and then, got into fights with the guys trying to buy weed off of my father. People would try to rob my father of money while buying weed because my father would give people weed on credit. I had to throw up some big dudes against the wall, and they were double my size. I didn't know where the strength came from.

If people cannot afford to pay now, then they probably will not be able to pay you back later.

If you choose to give, give; do not lend, or you will lose many relationships.

I learned how to understand the Jamaicans speaking patois because I would hang out with them playing dominoes, watching the horse races. They would get all excited and yell, "Go, jockey, go, jockey, go!" slamming down the dominoes on the table.

It was a good time. I ate well. My father would cook and we would get sandwiches with his EBT card. I got treated well. I was having a good time. I was young, and I didn't know what I was doing or how these things would affect me. Smoking weed was the least of my worries.

Then I started taking a pouch of weed when I went to Brooklyn. I would smoke with my friends and began to slow down, hanging out with my father. My father was not the nicest guy. I guess that is why people robbed him when he gave them credit. No one wants to help someone who is rude and nasty.

I then started calling my friends names, telling them, "Shut your c—," "Don't speak," and "Shut the f—up." I was talking to people this way based on what I learned through my father. He was a professional a—hole, and I learned how to be like him. You become who you associate with.

As kids, we respect our parents to a certain extent and start doing what they do, innately.

By this point, my friends didn't like me anymore. I started staying in Harlem, and my two friends got girlfriends. They didn't want to hang out. I started getting high with other people in Brooklyn instead of my father and my original friends. I had begun hanging out with a Spanish kid, Von, one of the kids from Brick Street in Brooklyn. He had his two little sisters in the living room, and we would go into his room, open the window, and smoke out the window. One day I was going to the pizzeria, and I ran into Rob, who was not my friend at that time. I barely knew him. He was pretty mean to me when we were in eighth grade. When we played football, he made fun of me because I was not good, but I didn't really take it seriously. He had seen me while he was with his sister. He smoked weed, so we ended up going to his house to smoke. I started hanging out with the Brick Street kids. Everybody knew I always had weed, and Rob would mimic me and say, "Got Dutch?" They said that's what I always said. We would all smoke the weed I had brought.

I sold weed for the first time one day while walking down the block with my friend Chris. It was a nice sunny day. I always had a little sack on me.

We ran into one of Chris's friends on the block. He asked Chris, "Do you know where I could get some weed?"

Chris said, "My boy right here got a little bit of weed. Jay, do you have something to sell him?" and I sold him something. Then we went to hang out and smoke.

I gave him my weed and told him to take out a bud.

He took out this giant piece of bud. I was looking to see how much weed he would take. I thought, "Oh, dude, maybe he doesn't know. Maybe he doesn't care. Maybe he just wants to get high." But it seemed as if he was going to try to take advantage of me.

He was a good kid with the most heart. He was good at anything he did. We were all poorly influenced by our parents, though, and we did not pay attention to if what we were doing was wrong or right.

I started learning how to sell weed. Then it got worse from there. I would bag up any extra weed from my pop's house and take it to Brooklyn to sell it. Now, when I smoked with people, I would ask them for some money. One time we were hanging out with this girl, Jasmin. She really liked me when we were in elementary school. Now, she had a boyfriend, and I think she might have been pregnant at that time.

We were all hanging out: Jasmin, her friend, Auto, and Chris. We were drinking beer, which I had never had before. I asked if he had something to chip in for weed. He did not, so he gave me this thing called a football, which is half of a Xanax. I was like, "What is this? What am I supposed to do with this?"

I didn't know how to get rid of it, so I ate it.

I started doing drugs from that moment. That was the beginning of the downfall.

One small habit can change your whole life.

I started popping Xanax regularly and learned how to sell it. I started selling weed on a larger scale. I would buy my own quarter pound and bring it to the neighborhood. I went down a dangerous lifestyle path. What triggered me to start selling weed on a larger scale was an altercation with my father. I came home from school after traveling one hour each way to live with this guy.

When I came home, the house was clean. He saw something on the floor and said, "Look at this!" yelling and getting upset about something for me to clean up.

I said, "Yo, you are home all day. Why don't you clean it up?"

I was on the Lazy Boy rocking chair, and he picked up a cutlass, a machete, and swung it at my face.

Thank God the Lazy Boy was a rocking chair. I rocked back, and the blade passed right in front of my face, one or two centimeters away from my cheek.

As soon as it passed my face, he dropped the machete and said, "I'm so sorry!" and tried to apologize.

That was it. I said, "F—you." I went and grabbed my PlayStation 2 and my clothes. I told him, "I come all the way here to be with you, and you do this." Before I left, I said, "I am never coming back here."

I went back the next week, though.

But at that point, I didn't feel safe living with him. That is when I really started selling more weed, getting into more drugs, and even selling Xanax. My friend's mom would sell me a whole case of Xanax for much cheaper than anybody else. Later, when I got older, about seventeen or eighteen, I would get ecstasy cheaper than anybody else. We tried ecstasy for the first time in the summer while we were gambling and playing cee-lo. We followed the ecstasy with some Xanax shortly after. I made a lot of money that night. I didn't even remember earning it. When I woke up, I saw that, apparently, I made a mess in the bathroom. I was f—ed up, but I woke up with money in my pocket. I had won in gambling.

The apple doesn't fall far from the tree.

I was going down the wrong path quickly. I got high often and took a lot of ecstasy. The first time, I chewed a G Lady, a triple stacker, and I swallowed a whole one. My friend Chris did the same thing. We had a crazy experience. We were bugging out at the family BBQ at our friend Ash's house, another Brick Street friend.

The trees were moving and vibrating. I remember thinking, "What the f—is happening? This is crazy."

All my friends were upset with me. Well, my friends at that time, they all blame me for us doing ecstasy.

I was stashing my weed in Rob's house and the night before Ash's BBQ, Rob's father told us not to come over there anymore. We would all get high, and messed up and leave the house a mess, making a whole bunch of noise, to the point that the neighbors would complain.

After the BBQ, we needed something to mellow us out. We needed the pot but didn't want to disturb Rob's father. Rob, Ash, and I went to Rob's house. They said, "You go up."

I went up through the front of the porch, climbed up to the second floor, and went in through the balcony door attached to Rob's room. My weed was in the safe. When I opened it up, I heard his father coming. I was heading out just as his father came in to search the room.

I ran off the balcony and jumped.

I jumped over the balcony's banister, and in midair, I turned around and grabbed onto the ledge. I inched myself down. I was so high off of ecstasy, I thought I could fly, I guess.

Thank God.

God swung me around. Otherwise, I would have fallen down three stories, all the way down to the basement.

I went back to the group and almost started up a fight with Chris and my sister's boyfriend's cousin. The night before, we were at my home, and he had been talking poorly about Chris, the one with the broken arm, saying he thought he was crazy, in a sort of a put-down way like what can he do with that broken arm. Chris was having problems with his family. He had recently put his hands through a glass window because of frustration. I was also having problems with my family. They had kicked me out of the house. I was living with my other friend Toms for the second time. At first, he had allowed me in, and this time, I was kind of forced to be there.

The first time, I was there because I was selling weed, and my mom didn't want me to sell weed in the house. I couldn't stay with my father. Toms and I teamed up, but he was never really that good of a businessman because he would want to smoke all of the profits and party. We never made money.

That's why I left there the first time. This time, I was stuck there. My mom saw my stash and took it. I came to her job and asked her, "Are you crazy? Where is my stuff? I owe someone money for that."

I didn't owe anyone money. I wanted my stuff back. She was upset, but she gave it back to me.

That is how my life was going. One day, after my family came back from Trinidad, I was in the park with friends when Rick, my sister's boyfriend, and his cousin had come there with my sister.

They all came and told me to come home. I said no, and my two friends told them, "Get out of here."

I left with my friends, drank, and got high, again.

What a bad habit I was stuck in. Sometimes these little choices grow to such a huge downfall.

Over time, I got better at selling weed. Eventually, I had three people running with me. I started off with Toms, Mike, and somebody I don't even remember. Then we started selling Xanax.

The human mentality is to get better at the things you do repeatedly.

One day while riding in Mike's car, we decided to go smoke in somebody's alleyway. I don't know what provoked us to do that.

That was another big mistake.

This was around the time when the drug-related arrests had started happening. I had been arrested once for weed, but because the cops knew my sister from working at a chicken place, they let me out with no problems. They didn't do anything to me.

I was going down this path—of being the bad kid—fast.

The world told me I was a bad kid, and I accepted it, instead of people helping me with perspective and feeding positivity into my life. I wish they had encouraged more positive activities to absorb all the excess energy.

That positivity was knocked out of me right there. My family aided in me, thinking that I was a bad kid once I started down this path. I'm not saying it was all their fault. It's because of the way I was nurtured, the things I was told, the way the system classified me. I ended up following that path because they said that's who I was. Many people around me, even my own mother, told me I would be just like my father.

Like Eminem says, "I am whatever you say I am. 'Cause if I wasn't, why would you say I am?"

We had a whole bunch of weed on us and a bag of Xanax. As Mike waited for us in the car in the driveway, Toms and I had robbed everything the workers had on them because that was how the game goes. We put all the knives and everything else in the car. We were robbing our own workers.

Toms and I weren't doing the best things.

We kept getting deeper into that world.

Four cop cars were parked out front. As we pulled out, one of them jumped on top of the car with the gun pointed toward us. When we got out of the car, they smashed us onto the floor. I tried to get on the floor as quickly as possible because I knew what was going to happen if I didn't.

This would be my second time getting arrested. They held me in jail for a night longer than everybody else because my mom had filed a PINS (person in need of supervision) petition against me. Everybody else got away. Mike got indicted with attempted murder for trying to run over the cop. It was dropped later on.

After I stayed that extra night, my mom and I had to sit in court together and talk to the judge before they would let me out.

I ended up going to school right near that central bookings later on, at Jay Street Metrotech.

Wow. How ironic, huh? Jail in a different form, serving time, maybe paying for my sins, or repenting. So close to one another, yet two different confining systems of life.

I cried that night in jail, wondering, "What am I doing here?" I thought I would never go back. I guess that one day was not enough.

I tried to stay home as long as I could, but my bad habits took over again. We are creatures of habit.

I was used to that life. I went right back into it. I would escape the house as much as I could and popped ecstasy any chance I had. The first day I escaped, my mom was trying to keep me in the house. She told me to stay home. I left, and she rode around looking for me. She saw me when she was driving the car back home, smacked me, and said, "Go back home."

I snuck back out and went to my friend Lui's house again, popped ecstasy, got high, and started down that path again. My mom couldn't control me. I couldn't control myself. I was on autopilot, heading to self-destruction.

I started hanging out with my original friends again.

The Brick Street Crew was doing robberies by then. I was not into it, but I was with them and backing them up. I was more into the fight and the thrill. One night, we robbed about six to eight people, beat up drunk Mexicans, and did a whole bunch of things. As we were robbing this innocent kid, he was like, "Hey, don't I know you?"

That same night, I saw my best friend, Sam, whom I hadn't seen in what felt like years. We were really messed up and tried to rob him because we could not even see what he looked like.

He woke us up, but we kept it moving. That same night, when we were robbing the last kid, one of these innocent kids walking home, I started to distance myself and was walking away. I didn't want to be a part of it. Then I saw four cars coming up the wrong way with no lights on. I said, "Hey, cops, cops."

My father always told me, "Anything you do in life, do it with confidence." Even if it's bad, do it with confidence, or you will get caught. I think that's a good suggestion if you're doing something good.

When you do anything, do it with confidence.

I walked right toward the cops, lit up a cigarette, and acted like I didn't know anything. They wrote about me in the newspapers: the one that got away.

All three of my friends got arrested.

I came back and hung out with them again. I had told one of the kid's girlfriends that he got arrested and that he was hanging out with that group and had popped Xanax. She didn't know. He wasn't supposed to be doing any of that.

So I looked like a rat.

No matter how much I tried to get away, trouble just kept happening over and over, like a bad cycle. One day I was walking home and bumped into these kids Ant and Chris. I was trying my hardest to stay away. Chris's leadership and influence started to grow, and after he broke his wrist, he pointed people toward doing the robberies. We attempted a robbery that night. Chris said, "Let's do it," and I was about to. The only one who followed through was Ant. I was over it at that point. I walked away that day.

Chris was going down a bad rabbit hole himself. We were really messed up, popping pills all the time. We were influenced by our parents. They were not the best influences. They were doing the wrong things, but we didn't see how bad it was. We didn't realize what we were doing. When you are in it, you cannot always see clearly.

When you are in the game, the pressure is on, and you do not see everything.

GOING OUT WITH A BANG!

We had another wild night going out for this neighborhood girl's birthday. The girl didn't want to see Josh, one of the kids we were with that day. I was going to go anyway because I was into her, and it was a bus party. Birdie said I could come with Chris, but I didn't get to clip my fingernails, so I went home to clip them and get ready. We missed the bus because we were rolling some weed.

We bought a bottle of E&J and finished a $15 bottle in thirty minutes. I popped seven Xanax and smoked half of a blunt while heading to the city on the train. Smoking the rest of the blunt on the train, we opened the window because people were yelling at us.

We made it into the city in half an hour. Then we got off the train.

I had $100 in my pocket, weed, drugs, and everything that we needed.

God always gives us more than enough; we just have to learn to be content with what we have. If we want more, we have to be willing to work for it.

This guy in the middle of Thirty-Fourth Street pulled out a wad of cash in front of us, a whole bunch of hundreds, right in front of me. I was like, what the hell is wrong with him?

I asked my friend Chris for the knife, and I went up to the guy and said, "Hey, give me $100." I just wanted the $100 for two packs of cigarettes. He threw the hundred dollars at me.

The cops said Chris was the one that told him to give us everything. The guy threw a one-hundred-dollar bill at us and ran off.

We took the $100 bill and split it in the store.

When we came out, some guys saw us and said, "That's the kids right there."

They ran after us. We were booking it. I was so messed up that I was blacking out while running. I would wake up and be halfway to the ground, catching myself and kept going. It was crazy. One of the guys grabbed my arm and threw me to the ground. I yelled out because I knew Chris was going to get caught. I saw his pace and where the guys were. I told them to be careful because he had recently broken his hand, and his hand was still messed up.

We got arrested, and they brought us to the precinct. I was so high that they didn't even find the drugs in my pocket. I put the bag of Xanax in my sock, then I put it in between my butt cheeks, then I threw it outside of my cell. When I was exiting the cell heading to Rikers Island, I saw the Xanax bag on the floor, and I picked it up and put it in between my butt cheeks again. Addictions.

While I was sleeping in the first cell, they woke me up, and I didn't even realize Chris was there.

They put him in a different cell. When I woke up, they pulled me out of the cell and tried to make me confess, and I told them I did everything. I wrote out my confession and everything.

I was so out of it. They caught me off guard. I didn't even know how to play the game. I didn't even know how to lie. I was not used to this life.

I never thought about getting into this life, yet I must have by the actions I was taking. Where else would my actions take me?

Your actions dictate your future. It is only a matter of time.

I confessed everything. I said, "I was the one that asked Chris for the knife. He had nothing to do with it."

Even in the paper, I wrote that we've never tried to hurt anybody. I just told him to give me the money. I never put the knife toward him. I never tried to get close to him with the knife. I just said, "Give me the money."

I didn't try to threaten his life. I got charged with first-degree robbery for saying that.

When they took me to Rikers Island, I had around thirteen Xanax left because I had taken seven. While waiting in the holding cell, I popped all thirteen of them. One of the other guys waiting said I fell asleep on the bench like a cockroach with my legs and hands up.

Another rabbit hole. When I was there, getting acquainted with some real thugs, I met this guy named Zook York. We went through the entry process together.

During the strip search, they made us squat down.

If I hadn't taken the pills, they would have definitely fallen out. They had us butt naked, crouching down to see if anything would fall out. I was naked in front of three other guys as a seventeen-year-old kid who had never had sex despite offers from so many beautiful women. I didn't get to experience the good side of being bad and taking drugs. I didn't get to experience the fun with women and partying the way I could have. All I did was drugs.

Make the most out of every experience. Go all out and do not hold back.

I ended up in the mod one. Chris and I slept side by side for five days. I didn't really do anything. I slept in my bed the whole time. Our Friday in the mods, the first black president of the United States was elected, President Obama. I didn't try to make a phone call. I gave Zook my information so he could use my phone card because he was kind of pressing me, and I didn't think I needed it. I wasn't even trying to be there. I thought that Friday when we went to see the judge, I would be going home, but my bail was fifteen grand. My family could not afford that at that second. My mom had to go and take it out of her 401(k).

I remember one guy threw a bar of soap at my head at night because I was always sleeping. I guess they were talking about me. I didn't care. I didn't listen to anybody.

My friend Chris got bailed out, and I ended up staying in jail. I went to South One, a different unit, and I started connecting with the Muslim community because it was its own gang in there.

My mother's Muslim; my father's Hindu. I was raised Muslim because my mom raised us, so I started going to mosque and praying. I had protection now, thanks to this one guy whose cell was next to mine. He made me ramen noodles with crushed up Cheez-It and tuna.

It was banging, super good.

When I came home, I had asked my mom to make it for me again.

One of my experiences in jail for those twenty days was when I broke down and I started crying. I thought to myself, *Jay, you were going to be a doctor. How are you wasting your life right now?* I was wasting my life, stuck in a cell.

I'd rather be poor and free than rich and caged. I'd rather be rich and free more than both of those options.

I was on the verge of switching over my mindset in jail and starting to plant my flag there. I started cleaning up my room. I kept the bathroom clean. I began doing push-ups because I was getting weak. After those five days, I started to eat every day.

After realizing that I was going to stay here, I decided to become good at this too. It is human instinct to want to become good at anything you do. I was going to become good at being in jail. I was doing push-ups, socializing, getting into the rhythm and lifestyle. I didn't think my mom had fifteen grand to bail me out. One day, I called the house, and my little sister answered. She told my family what happened, but I didn't speak to anybody after that call. I called from the mosque phone. Before I even went to the first cell at Rikers, I called my friend Biggs and told him I was getting arrested. I guess Biggs and I were close.

I was playing cards with the other prisoners. I was getting acquainted and knew I was going to fight if I had to fight.

One time, this guy tried to take my Patackies. I told him, "Nah, I'm good." My Muslim friend tried to stand up for me. I told him, "Nah, I'll stand up for myself. Thank you."

I told the first guy pressing me, "Get out of here." I was a scrawny kid. He was a little, skinny pimp. The guy was in there for two gun charges. He had shot somebody at the Labor Day parade. Later on, he lent me his book. He was a nice dude because I stood up for myself.

When I went to court on the twentieth day, my mom came. She told my uncle who had just come from Trinidad what happened. He said, "Get him out of there." The next day, she bailed me out.

When I was going to go spend some money at the commissary and buy food, I realized someone had deposited money for the commissary, but I didn't know who.

After I bought food, I heard I was getting bailed out later that day. I was in my room, and these two gangsters were trying to break into my cell for my commissary. That's when I saw the COs were corrupt because they were going to open the door for them. The dude wanted two packs of ramen noodles and some tuna. I gave it to him. I told him to get out. I was really scared, though. I was planning to lay on the bed, and when they tried to attack me, I was going to kick them in the face.

There were two of them. They were the two biggest predators in there. One of them literally looked like the Predator. They were both Spanish, yet I thought they were black until they spoke.

When I was praying, I remembered Botz coming up to us. When I was in the cell, Botz had just got arrested too, he was a kid from the neighborhood. He said, "Jay, can you guys protect me? Can I become Muslim?"

I guess that is why many people become Muslim in jail.

One time this guy aggressively slid into our prayer trying to disrupt us, when four of us were praying in the corridor.

I was about to kick him in his head, but I didn't want to get in trouble. I didn't know my limitations. I wasn't trying to get sent to any box. Connecting with the Muslims helped me during my time in jail.

That day I was leaving, I gave away the rest of the commissary. Thank God I was leaving because if I had stayed, I would have been herbed for giving those two some food. Then I gave the rest of my food away to somebody when I was leaving and clearing out my cell. You never feel safe until you actually leave the building, so I didn't know if I was getting out. I didn't even call my mom when I got out.

Thank God my mom put up the bail money.

My mentality was sure going to change after I was in there.

The day I got out, I went to visit Biggs. I used the phone at the store where we buy Dutches, but he didn't answer.

On my way home, for some reason, I was so scared of everything around me. I thought some kids were coming after me at one point, and I hid on somebody's stoop.

Jail was a crazy experience. Reflecting back, I didn't realize how scared I was.

When I made it home, my mom had made burgers and coleslaw, my favorite.

The way my family was looking at me, I could tell they were so disappointed in me.

I went and took a shower, and I shaved off all my hair, including my beard and underarm hair. I had only showered about three to four times in the twenty days I spent there. I would also keep clean in my room a bit as well with a rag, just wiping up my armpits. I came out, and we ate. They still loved me, but I knew they were upset.

I thought I had gotten rid of all my drugs, but I knew I still had some Xanax in one of my pants. I thought they threw them out.

"Oh, you threw out the pants. I had some drugs in there," I told my mom. "Thank God you threw them out. I was looking for them to get rid of them anyway."

A week or two later, I found the drugs in another pair of pants.

I didn't have any money. My mom was willing to give me a few dollars, but I didn't really care for it.

I have always made my own money since I was fifteen. So I ended up taking those Xanax pills, and I gave them to a kid I knew to sell for me. When he started selling for me, I'd make forty to eighty bucks each flip.

I started getting more for him to sell, and then somebody robbed him. I told him, "Don't worry about it."

Soon, I started going back into the lifestyle again. I started selling weed with my first girlfriend. We had six runners with us. We were probably doing more work than everybody else, but it was more volume and a higher percentage of pay.

We grew our team, but we were doing the brunt of the work.

I ended up getting back into all the same stuff again.

Coming out was there ever going to be a change?

As I came out of jail, I came home to love and burgers. The next day, I was going to school and getting acclimated again.

The first teacher I saw was Ms. Vee, who said she cried about me. She saw where my transcripts were sent. She was happy to have me back. I returned, and I passed every test they gave me.

When I was in jail, I realized that I was seventeen, had done all these drugs, but never had any girl and never had sex. That got to me. I thought, *Damn, I've been playing around with drugs all my life. I haven't even gotten to connect with a girl.*

So that day, I pulled four girls in one shot, two from one group of friends, one from another group, and one more. I took them up to my friend Biggs's building. I called, but he didn't answer. I took them up to his staircase, where he used to live. He had already moved to the next side of the building. The girls and I went up there, rolled up a blunt, and started smoking. We were all getting high. I had never really hung out with girls intentionally before. That showed me how powerful we are. When you really want something, you could make it happen quicker than you think.

Pure intention and determination can help you manifest anything you put your mind to.

I had two classes with the first girl I started talking with. So we had connected through the classes. I was talking to her before I had gotten arrested. I took her downstairs because she had to leave. Her father was calling her; she was in trouble for something. I think she had taken weed or pills from him.

I walked her down the block, and then I came back upstairs to the girls, and that was pretty much it. The lady Dee, an older woman I know I could have, saw me and was like, "I don't want to do my laundry. I want a reason not to do laundry." She was putting it out there for me to convince her not to do the laundry and do something else. I guess I was still scared. I thought she was beautiful. I didn't hear the best stories about her, but she was hot to me. I guess I may have been intimidated. The other two girls, we talked for a little bit, and then we all split up. I started to hang out with that one girl that I walked down the block, Missy.

I went to Missy's house two or three times after school. She invited me to come over and smoke in her bathroom. Then one day, her friend Trina, whom I shared a class with for three years, said, "Jay, you know she has a boyfriend?" in front of Missy. Missy looked at me as if to say, "Damn this girl."

I was shocked. I didn't even know where this was going anyway. I was working on hanging out with girls. This was all a new experience for me.

I left a little while after and kept it moving.

She was around me a lot after that. We got out of school around the same time. One day, I brought her to my brother's house. We smoked and started making out. We started hooking up even though I knew she had a boyfriend. One day, she was supposed to meet with him, and she didn't because she was with me. He was getting angry apparently, but she didn't tell me anything. I said, "Let me walk you home."

It was day time. I walked her to her corner. I had already met her parents in passing. She told them I was just a friend from school, I didn't want them to think anything.

Apparently, as I was walking away, her boyfriend came up to her with a knife and started threatening her, she told me later on. She told me she wanted to break up with him. He had cheated on her and videotaped it, trying to get her upset. She wanted to break up with him, but he wouldn't let her break up; he would always call her and harass her. While we were in our economics class, she said, "This guy keeps harassing me, and he won't leave me alone."

We sat right next to each other. We would even join our table together, which was not recommended by our teacher. I took my phone, and I went downstairs to the bathroom. I called him and tried to be very nice at first. I said, "Hey, can you leave this girl alone?" He didn't want to hear that. I ended up having to threaten him a little bit.

I said, "Hey, I know who you hang out with. I know where you hang out. Leave this girl alone, or me and you are going to have problems."

I went to the park where he hung out and I didn't see him. I was not scared of anybody at this point. I had no fear in my heart, especially after being in jail and being free. Even since I was younger, I never worried, and nothing really fazed me. I knew I could handle the consequences of whatever came my way.

Missy and I started going out. We were not officially dating; it was more like hanging out. She had three or four hot friends, and I had two or three friends for them. We hung out together often, drinking and smoking, and would go party in my cousin's basement. My aunt used to care for a lady upstairs.

We all popped ecstasy, but my cousin did not know.

My friend Jack had a three-way kiss with two beautiful girls.

Trina, which was one of the girls there, said, "Hey, you know, when you pop ecstasy, you usually can't get it up."

Missy and I were anticipating having sex. I knew I was going to have sex that night. I had popped ecstasy before but never had to deal with this problem. Trina was right. I got nervous. My blood was still flowing, but it wasn't working. Maybe because it was my first time as well. From there, we were in the bathtub, all over the place.

My friends had left already. The girls were sleeping in my cousin's bed. I was in the back bedroom with Missy, where my little cousin used to sleep. I couldn't complete the transaction. I called my friend Jack at three or four in the morning and told him, "Yo, bro, you won't believe what happened," and told him the situation.

The next time that we drank and smoked with the girls, we were walking to the pizzeria, and Missy said, "Hey, you guys walk that way. We're going to walk this way."

We went around the block without them, and as we walked down the block, she came directly in front me and stopped me dead in my tracks.

She was about 5'2", and I was 5'10". She looked up at me and said, "Hey, do you want to be with me? Or do you want me to stand on the sideline while you f—my friends?"

I thought, *This girl is wild.* I turned around and looked up at the moon, and she went to sit on a stoop. I was going through a lot of stress for court and trying to see how things would turn out with my court case, whether I would go to jail for years or get probation.

When I turned back around, she was standing right in front of me and put me on the spot. I said, "I guess."

We started going out from then on. The next day, after school, we went back to her house with this guy named Vinny, who was a good friend of hers.

On the way there, I saw my friend Toms on the corner looking at me. I said, "Give me two weeks and I'm done. I'm out," meaning I would hit it and be out.

Then I brought her, and Vinny back to my place. I had this dresser covered with a mirror as the barrier, creating my room in the living room. We smoked a bit, and then Vinny left.

I thought she was going to give it up to me.

She said, "I am on my period," so that didn't happen. She treated me really nice. She was trying to win me over. Then a week later, at her house, I had sex for the first time. It took me six months of energy to get results.

This is why most men are not successful until after forty: because they have chased women.

The sex was good. We both enjoyed it. It was in her parents' bed. I just plopped down and laid back. We were both tired.

She looked at me. I don't remember how it came up, if she said something or if I said something. She realized it was my first time having sex. She was like, "What? I would have never known."

That same week, she started telling me she loved me. That was a crazy shock. I started saying it back.

This was my senior year. Each time she knocked on my classroom's door, somebody would open it. She'd bring me a plastic bag with cut up strawberries, a sandwich, Polly-O cheese, and chocolate milk, kiss me on my cheek, and leave. This was in Ms. Vee's class, where I spent four years. Missy showed me what love was.

Soon as she closed the door, my teacher, Ms. Vee—my favorite and most consistent teacher, would say, "Jay, I told you about that. Stop having that girl come to my classroom."

That was life.

My friend Reggie told me that she was with one of his friends, John.

I didn't believe him because I was so infatuated with this girl.

Our rocky journey started there. We would hang out together with a whole bunch of other people. The a-hole that I learned to be from hanging out with my father, she got the brunt of that. I'd tell her to shut the f—up in front of everybody, and she would shut up. She was the captain of the basketball team. I never saw her play a single ball game. I wasn't as supportive as I could have been at first.

She accepted me for who I was, and no matter how I treated her, she treated me well, creating a safe environment for me to heal and change. She gave me unconditional respect and love.

I was still trying to get out of the streets but still stuck there. I thought I had gotten rid of all of my pills and all my drugs, but I had found sixty Xanax pills, which was worth $300 at retail cost. I ended up making about $180 off of it and helping another dude make $100.

I had him continue to sell for me and made money every week. I did not go back to selling weed at first, but I started again. When Missy and I started going out, I had my friend Sam, Jack, Biggs, Toms, Jonathan, and Josh. A whole bunch of people sold with me. We were making a few bucks, decent money. I worked at the car wash once, for two weeks, maybe a month. But selling is how I supported myself since I was 15.

When my birthday came around, I got sentenced to the CASES (Center for Alternative Sentencing and Employment Services) program, which included six months of drug tests to see how I would behave and follow the rules.

When I came out after getting arrested, I heard that people were saying I was a rat. I told Chris exactly what I told the cops: I asked him for the knife, but he didn't know what I was going to do with it. I wrote this all out in the paper.

I tried to take the blame, but saying he had the knife and that I took it from him is what made him an accessory to the crime. He had three cases pending against him, two others that I wasn't involved with. By the time I came home, he had told many people that I was a rat. My brother and sister worked around the neighborhood, and my brother said, "Jay, people are calling you a rat. You better go talk to that kid."

When my brother tells me I have to do something, I have to do it. I saw Chris at school.

I was in my gym uniform. I had left class to go use the bathroom. I saw him, and I ran up to him.

"Hey, what's up? I hear you guys are calling me a rat. What happened?" I asked him. "You know exactly what I said. I told you what I said."

He said, "Yeah, but what you wrote on the paper was not right."

"Yeah, but I had already written it, and what could I do?"

He was like, "Yeah, yeah…" and after talking a while, we went and smoked a blunt at Toms' house with Josh again.

We never talked after that.

He started calling me later on and making threatening phone calls. I was a little scared of him. I can't lie. I was hearing crazy stories about what they were doing on the Block, and I had too much to live for. I remember he was wild in his own way; it was the way we were raised. It was our nurturing and our nature. We were not in the right situation.

People did not allow us to change back to being good because they had already classified us as bad. We filled those shoes. Coming back home this time, my family gave me an environment to become a good person again.

I understood I had to take responsibility for my actions.

They didn't say anything specific to me. They allowed me to grow into myself in my own way, at my pace. Later on, they made a few comments about my past. They paid my bail, so maybe they wanted to make sure they got back that $15,000.

Chris and I didn't connect at all. These threats just created more tension. When our court case got split up, everybody really thought I was a rat. After coming out, I never went back to the block. I told myself I was never going back to Brick Street. I had finally decided that I wasn't going back to that life.

I never stepped back onto that block until I was twenty-two. I didn't want to associate with them. I didn't care what they said about me.

Now, I'm hanging out with this girl, and we were having a good time. I started selling weed again with my friends. Before I got sentenced to CASES, I went to prom. I knew the court decision was coming up. I had rolled up twenty blunts for prom and put them in White Owl cases. My girlfriend and I had some regs (low-grade weed) and some high grade and mixed it up.

When I reached the prom, two tubes dropped down my pants leg and fell onto the ground. I saw a Dean looking at it. When he picked it up and was about to open it, I said, "Hey, that's mine."

I grabbed it out of his hand, and he let me go. He was like, "Oh, okay."

He might have known what it was but didn't look inside. Officer Diego, a cop they had on the premises, knew me a bit. I had already smoked outside, twice. I smoked in places they told us not to smoke or hang out. I went back in, and Officer Diego came in as I was using the bathroom. I laughed in my head because I knew what was coming. He said some smart stuff, trying to see if I would incriminate myself.

I said, "What's up?"

We looked at each other, and both knew what was up. I walked out, smelling like weed.

After prom, we went to this bar called Illusions. We had the whole place and drank Amaretto sours and smoked inside. My girlfriend was dancing on top of me while I was sitting on the couch. The security came and told her to get off of me, yelling at us, "You guys cannot be doing that here." We were always all over one another, even on school days. She came over, or I went over to her place. We would smoke, f—, eat. That's all we did.

We laughed. I said, "Let's get out of here."

It was getting packed and rowdy, but not too crazy yet. This place was illegal. We were not even supposed to be there. When we went to leave, some person had just busted their head on the wall.

I said, "It's time to get out of here for real." As we walked downstairs, they were trying to keep us in the building because of the injury.

I told the security guard, "Yo, move."

I moved them out my way, grabbed my girl, and went back to the afterparty bus. We waited there. We saw the cops roll up on many people, but a lot of our friends got out. We went back to the house where we left our things, then we made it back to my home and smoked some Buddha.

She stayed over.

The first time that she fell asleep at my house was about two months into us going out. We woke up at like 11:00 p.m. I didn't want to walk her home. I was tired and said, "Just stay."

Her mom called at two in the morning.

"Jay, where's my daughter?"

I said, "Right here. She's on the couch in my sister's room. She was watching TV and fell asleep. Let me go get her." Missy picked up the phone.

Her mom started yelling, "Do you know what time it is?"

All she could say was, "I am sorry, sorry, sorry. I'm coming home right now."

I was like, "Oh my God. Give me the phone." She passed it to me.

"Hey, Nette, I'm sorry. She is sleeping on the couch in my sister's room," I said, giving her daughter dignity.

I said, "I really don't want to walk her home; it's two o'clock right now. Can she come home in the morning?"

She said okay. Every weekend since then, that girl slept over. She would technically say she was going to her friend Jessica's house. We went to Jessica's house sometimes and then ended up back at my house. When I was selling pot with all those guys and her, I was still popping Xanax a little bit longer. When CASES started, I stopped popping Xanax and smoking pot.

A NEW CHAPTER

I did well in CASES. I had started working at Nellie Bly amusement park, which became Adventurer's Park, while I was there. It was a theme park for kids that we had gone to since we were young. It was on the side of the highway before you reached Coney Island.

We started working there because Missy had worked there the summer before, and she helped me get a job. It gave me leeway from going into the CASES program every day. That summer, I got three shades darker and gained 50 pounds. When I came out of jail, I was 140. By the summer, I was 160, and by the end of the summer, I was 190 pounds. When we went school shopping, I called her over, saying, "What did you do to me?" referring to my weight going from 32 to 36.

I would walk this girl home knowing I shouldn't be out because it was after curfew. Because of CASES, I had to be at home by 8:00 p.m., but work sometimes finished at 10:00 p.m. A few of the youngsters tried to scare me sometimes and would speak nonsense when they saw me late at night.

I didn't let anybody get to me. I walked her home.

Then winter came, and they sentenced me to probation. Though I was supposed to be on probation for five years, they only kept me on for two years.

That first month I got sentenced for probation, I ended up smoking one of the biggest blunts I'd ever smoked, and by then, I hadn't smoked in a few months. I got super high and became paranoid about smoking too late at night. I worried about all these kids out there not liking me.

I was eighteen, and I was in college. I was about to get a job and was working to make a life for myself.

SUMMER 2009

Starting from the summer of 2009, when I worked at Nellie Bly, I stayed on that path of working, so I did not have to go to CASES daily. I wanted to make money and grow myself.

Since I couldn't smoke pot, I started popping ecstasy with Missy. I was getting it for $2 a pop from my brother's friend. That's when I started selling it. Ecstasy was going for five or six bucks wholesale. Retail cost was ten to twenty bucks. I could charge people a lot of money.

I usually sold it to a few people and partied with them. It was just paying for my supply, so I didn't have to worry about money or finding ecstasy. This allowed us to enjoy ourselves. One night I popped four of them. We would go crazy and have great times.

I was chubby. I don't know what these girls saw in me at Nellie Bly. This one girl came up to Missy and said something to the effect of "Your boyfriend is so fine." She came and told me and was very upset.

My mom and my sister were away for the summer. I can't remember where they went. I invited my girlfriend and five girls back to my house. I was the only guy, and we were all popping ecstasy. Two of them were lesbians.

We were all messed up. One girl had a boyfriend, but he was not there. She was a very loyal girl. The other girl named Scooby. She was beautiful. I thought she was hot. I was in love with my girl, though. I didn't really have eyes for anybody else. She was pretty, though, I could not lie.

We were all on the bed while my girlfriend was telling a story, relaxing. We were just chatting, nothing sexual. We all had our clothes on. Scooby was staring at me the whole time. I kept looking at my girlfriend, trying to ask her with my face, "Do you see this girl looking at me?"

She wasn't seeing. Then Scooby came out of her mouth and said, "Why are you looking at me?"

I said, "What? You are the one staring at me the whole time! I wasn't looking at you."

She was trying to play me in front of everybody, in front of my girlfriend. Like, what? You crazy.

I just thought that was a funny story.

When my girlfriend and I were having a little fight, I had mentioned her name, and she got upset about that. I know how to push people's buttons. It wasn't intentional; I just did it. I was being myself at that point in my life, but being me pushed buttons. I was blunt and straight up.

At the park, this guy, Eddie, the mechanic at the shop, used to say things about my girlfriend. He would say stuff like, "Oh, you know, I slept with your girlfriend."

He was a good-looking dude, I'm not going to lie. I didn't really care, but when he said that foul stuff in front of her though, that's when I got upset. Everybody liked my girlfriend. This other big brolic dude liked my girlfriend too.

To that guy, I said, "Didn't I tell you not to talk to her?"

Then the other guy, Eddie, I said to him, "Yo, why don't you come meet me after you get out of work. I would beat the crap out of you."

He hung out with kids that I was infamous among and people that didn't like me. That was his family. They would have beat me up. They could have tried at least. There would have been a lot of them. They came to pick him up from work that day. He ran out with a wrench, walking away as fast as he could. I was ready to kill him. Well, not kill him, but beat him up. I really didn't want to fight him. He was putting me in a situation where I had to fight. I was not really scared to fight. I wouldn't want to hurt anybody, but he was putting me in that position.

Stand up for yourself and others and especially for your loved ones.

After Chris got charged and sentenced, his father came by the job one day, but he didn't come in. We didn't speak. My friend Ash had come in to see what I was doing. He worked there for a day. He said, "Jay, what are you doing here working with all these clowns?"

We had a good life. My friends loved me in their own way. They knew I was not a rat because of how I came and spoke to Chris when I got out. I simply decided to go the right way.

Just shift. Make the changes necessary, even if you are leaving all you know behind. New horizons await you.

They had nothing else to call me because there was no reason for me not to go back to them; it was home. We were family. Even though we never said it. We spent most of our time together. We were the bad kids, so all the bad kids joined together.

Good people hang out with good people; bad kids hang out with bad kids.

You are who you associate with. Birds of a feather flock together.

That is why we have to be very careful about how we talk to and about people. For instance, my mom always told me I would be just like my father, and my family would speak that into me.

There is power in the spoken word and who you let speak into your life.

When I came back, I had signed up for college. Now you can laugh at me about how I registered. The CUNY system has you choose the five schools you want to go to, all at once. I chose them, but I didn't realize the first one that you choose is your top priority and the one you're most likely to get accepted to. I ended up going to John Jay College.

I had a good time. It was a great experience and the campus was nice. I remember one Spanish girl at the end of the year. We liked each other. We were taking ethnic studies. The class was a real challenge of the mind because we were breaking all the stereotypes we believed about each other. She would sit right next to me, and we would chat. She had a boyfriend, I had my girlfriend, but we really liked each other. One day she called me while I was with my girlfriend because we had exchanged numbers. I heard her voice, but I didn't save her number. She never called me back, and I lost her number at that point.

In that school, I did well. I had gotten all my credits. I got mostly As, one C, and one B. Economics really killed me because the teacher was not great, and it was Friday. My girlfriend loved to come see me in the city. It was an evening class. I got out at five. We were in love and saw each other every day before college started. We started college at the same time, and she also started working. We barely saw each other as much as we wanted.

Distance makes the heart grow fonder.

I always wanted to get out of the class early because I knew she was waiting for me. I didn't do well in that class. I ended up leaving that school to transfer to City Tech for chemical technology. That year, my girlfriend and I really connected.

We started hanging out with Sam again. I got my first job outside of Nellie Bly. I went on a few interviews, including H&M and Buy Buy Baby. I got the interview at H&M because of a case manager. I had graduated with high honors from the six-month CASES program, where they gave me a $500 scholarship to pay for my laptop. I got hired at Buy Buy Baby.

According to the law of inertia, a body in motion says in motion.

I got in the mode of working and placed strong new habits in my life.

I was diligent. I was ready to change my life. I wanted to become better, but breaking habits is hard.

We are creatures of habits.

The more positivity I put in my life, the less time I had for nonsense.

That is how I changed my habits. I prioritized what was more important and put more positive activities and challenges on my plate.

I didn't really like working at Buy Buy Baby at all. It was a boring place. It was nice, but it just wasn't any fun. It was so mundane. I was selling baby products, and they put me in the hardest section. They would ask me, "Oh, why are you taking so long to do your work?" I didn't even understand why they'd put me in the hardest section, then ask me why I was taking so long. It didn't make sense to me.

After two weeks, they called me into the office. I was doing my job. If you tell me to do something, I'm going to do it and do it good too, to the best of my abilities. These two guys pulled me into a room, looked at me, and sat on both sides of me. I had rage pent up inside of me from the lifestyle change, getting rid of all my poor habits like smoking weed, drinking, and popping pills. That year, I stopped cigarettes as well.

I hadn't completed the journey yet, because I was still popping ecstasy once in a blue. After the summer, that was it for a while.

These guys sat down, looked at me for a while, and said they were going to have to let me go.

When I was sitting there, I thought about punching both of them in their head at the same time.

They did not fire me nicely. They had no emotion. They did not give me any reasons. They didn't explain themselves. They just fired me.

You know what? I didn't care.

Actually, I really did care, but I just left. I walked out, and I started crying as I walked down the block. Man, I was just trying to do the right thing. I called my girlfriend. I felt really down.

The next week H&M called me. I loved that job. I had a lot of fun and met a lot of cool people and beautiful women. It was in the heart of the city, Thirty-Fourth Street and Seventh Avenue. The same station I had got off the day I got arrested. I enjoyed working there. I asked for twenty to twenty-five hours, and they would give me thirty-eight hours. They were working me like a dog because I worked so hard. I used to come in a little high. I was still on probation, but they only drug-tested me through mouth swabs. I learned how to pass the test by gargling Listerine right before you take the test. I would smoke the night before and still pass.

I was still smoking every day after college. I would even smoke before school sometimes. I didn't really care to smoke before I did my work, but I would when I worked at H&M. I stopped enjoying work because they worked me hard. Eventually, I hated going. But I would smoke beforehand, and I would be super focused and kill it. They'd put me in the worst section. I would make that whole section immaculate in a matter of twenty to thirty minutes. I would run the clothes back and put everything back where it belonged. I tried to maintain my section for the rest of that time, to not have to worry at the end of my shift. They ended up giving me more duties to handle because I would do mine so quickly. After my first review, they wanted to make me a supervisor or manager within six months.

As soon as I heard that, something went off inside of me. I didn't want to be a manager there. And I wanted to get out even more. I started rebelling and calling out of work more often, especially after they denied my request to have three or four days off, not even popular days, one weekend, several months in advance I had been there for over six or seven months.

I went on the trip for as long as I could. I drove back early and saw my nephew when I came home. I was watching him and said that I didn't want to go to work. I called out those days anyway, even though I cut my trip short.

My nephew was born the first year I got out of jail. Thank God I got to love on him. He stayed at the house, and while we nurtured him, he nurtured me back to life. This allowed less room for me to engage in too much nonsense. I was working. I was going to school and loved watching him.

I was putting many positive things into my life that I didn't have room for the negativity. My nephew taught me a lot. He loved me a lot because, when I spend time with anybody, I focus on them. I spend time and connect with them. As my mentor says, if you treat anyone like a number, treat them like number one.

Before my nephew could even talk, I remember a day he was in the kitchen with three of us. I think I was with my sister and my girl-friend and someone said, "Who do you love the most?" He pointed at me; he couldn't even speak yet. I was on the side, not even right in front of him.

That was the relationship I had with him.

I hung out with him as much as I could while he was young. From the day I saw him taking his first steps, I would tell my nephew and any kids—and make sure they knew—they could be or do whatever they want, and I will help you do or become it. When I said that to him, it internally came back to myself.

I thought to myself, *Wow, Jay, you were once that little kid. You could do whatever you want.*

What you put out is what you get back.

You can live out your dreams.

Go after what you want. Yeah, sure, you will go through your challenges. Don't let them become detrimental. You can have your dreams; you decide where you go. I learned that from watching a little kid walk for the first time. You can do whatever you want with your life.

I was working hard. I partied one time for my girl's birthday because it was my best friend's birthday the same day. I rented out a hookah lounge section. Everybody popped ecstasy except Sam's brother and Sam's friend. I was selling ecstasy to everybody there. We were in the VIP lounge and were not supposed to be there because we weren't twenty-one, but I had talked with the manager beforehand, and he just gave it to me. It was called Nirvana, right across from the Sahara. We had a great time.

I had this sweet, chill, no-nonsense, hardworking, smart vibe. I was good-looking, and even though I was chubby, I was feeling myself. I had swagger, and having a beautiful girl around your arm didn't hurt.

My mindset was being built. I was remembering who I was. I was rebuilding myself. Since seventh grade, when I went to Trini, up until then, I had forgotten who I was. I had forgotten all the important things that I had done, the ambition, hard work, and that I wasn't scared to work. I took things for granted and became casual about life.

That's how I became a casualty.

I completed my first year at John Jay. I was getting through probation. Everything was going good in my life. I was about to transfer schools.

I went to City Tech because they had a hospitality management program. That's what I studied in high school. I liked it. It had a cool vibe. I must have been drawn to that field for a reason, but after the transfer was completed, the program was filled.

Now, I had to choose a curriculum. What to choose? While I was talking to my probation officer, she said, "Jay, you don't need a degree to become a hotel manager. Why don't you challenge yourself?"

I thought, *How could I challenge myself?*

I thought back on my life. I passed every class in high school.

The only Regents test I failed was chemistry. I passed the class because the teacher liked me, and I helped her file her paperwork for twenty school service hours. And the tests were easy. For the Regents, you had to know more details on each subject. So I chose chemical technology as my major.

At first it was a big adjustment.

I was still working thirty-eight hours but getting As. I really got upset with my managers. I told them, "Hey, when I first came here, I said I only wanted twenty-five hours max, and you guys keep giving me thirty-eight hours. I talked to you guys twice. I need to sit down with somebody."

I never really took nonsense. The only reason I took thirty-eight hours was that I didn't mind working. I liked working, but after they didn't grant me my vacation, I saw they really didn't care about me. They were more concerned with what I could do for them, which I realize more now.

A wise lady once told me, "Don't let them steal your youth, Jay."

And that's what made me think about the job differently. You can't tell me I can't go somewhere. I'm working, busting my butt, and you are going to tell me I can't go away for a few days? I wasn't even asking for them to pay for my days off. They had a whole six weeks' notice about this.

I started treating jobs like that. You are not going to steal my youth. That's the same way I think of it now. You're not going to steal my life and dreams away from me for a paycheck. I will take care of my responsibilities. There are so many ways to make money. Don't play with me.

I got back into hustling a little bit, selling weed, still being influenced by hanging out with my father. My father was going through a lot of troubles while I was working at H&M. He got arrested eight times that year. He wasn't seeing me as much because I was with my girlfriend all the time, not visiting him. We had our experiences. He should know that I didn't want to hang out with him and that he was a bad influence in my life at that point.

I had to become stronger so I could actually help him. I couldn't help him being there with him. He and I would smoke, and I would stray. I didn't have time for it. I would still smoke on my own, but not the way we used to smoke. One of those eight times he was arrested, I bailed him out once. I took him to the courthouse to pay the money. He had $300 in his pocket, and it just vanished.

I don't know what he did with it. He is probably a genius, or maybe he lost it. I searched this guy's whole person. I checked every single pocket. He had no money, nothing. Wow. I couldn't figure how this guy did this.

I had given him the $300. He said he would pay me back, but he never did. My brother got upset about that. Later, he got arrested again. He called me. "Jay, I have no money. I just came home from jail," blah, blah, blah.

I thought, *Oh my God. This guy is annoying.* It was too much. I was the only one out of all my siblings dealing with him and trying to help him. I called my brother and said, "Hey, Sean, I really need your help, man. I need you to come over here and see your father. I will go with you, but I'm tired of going by myself. I need your support.

He agreed. I told him to pick up my girlfriend when he was coming. I told her to get a $50 sack of weed. I was going to give my father some weed. I knew he wouldn't have weed because the cops took it all.

I got over there, and it broke my heart. He wasn't doing well. We fought about him being on crack for a while. I told him at one point, as we were walking back from this program, and I was still popping ecstasy. So maybe it was because of what I was doing, popping ecstasy once in a while. I popped it for my girlfriend's birthday when I bought her a Coach purse because I had taken hers at an event.

The night before I got arrested, I went to a Halloween party, and she was there. I didn't know she was going to be there. We had met up and talked earlier that day. I didn't know she had a boyfriend at that time, Rex. She had a new boyfriend three or four months later.

Everybody at the party was robbing people. That was what we were surrounded by, so I took a purse. I walked out with a Coach purse. I didn't even know what Coach was. I looked in the purse. It looked like someone had already stolen from the purse. Inside of it was a Razor phone and a broken watch. I took the purse and threw it in the air, gave the Razor phone to my friend's grandmother, and I kept the watch.

When I came back to class from jail, we had a class together. This was before we went out. She said, "Jay, you know anybody who robbed a purse? It had this and that."

Once she described what it had inside, in my head, I was like, "Yeah, I saw that." But some other stuff was missing already. That's how I knew somebody else robbed it. I said no.

But six months later, she was hanging out at my house. I already put the watch in my sister's room. I got it and said, "Hey, you recognize this?" That was funny. She told me that I stole her purse before I stole her heart.

I was doing really good, taking care of my father, and helping him through his situation. I was still partying after school and work. I still found time for that. That's why I kept getting fat and stayed fat. I didn't make time for anything else good for myself. I would do my work at school and my job, but to deal with work, I used those substances instead of getting stronger. I would use them to help keep me calm and get through the day and life, to numb my mind and not think so much. Weed brings you to compassion because it slows you down. The ego can either shrink or grow, but it was shrinking for me.

I became more self-aware.

I digressed. My brother picked up my girl, then came to pick me up from work at H&M, so we could go to our father's house.

I walked in first, and I turned my face and saw this big fat guy with this scrawny little black woman and my father.

My father's pants were down. His eyes were bulging out his face. All of them were high off crack.

I was so upset, man. It was so sad. He couldn't even answer me. He couldn't even pull up his own pants. My brother walks in after me. I said, "Sean, watch this guy for a second. I'm coming right back."

I took my girl outside because this crack dealer and the crackhead were in my father's house. I didn't know if the cops were going to come and wasn't trying to get my girl in trouble. I took her outside and took the weed and put it in the trunk of the car.

I told Sean to go outside and wait with my girl. Damn, my brother really had my back, and he wasn't scared to listen to me.

I was disappointed with my father. I felt so bad because that day I had walked him home from his program, the day I bought my girlfriend the Coach purse, I asked him, "Pops, what can I do, man? I'll do anything for you. I will carry you on my back. Can you stop this, please?"

He said, "Yeah." He just kept going back to it.

I was telling him what to do, and I wasn't watching what I was doing. Even though I had a job and went to school, I was still doing some wrong things.

I saw this guy high, and I was so beat up seeing him like that. He is my father, and he couldn't even function; he acted like everything was a joke. It was probably the same self-defense mechanism I had, laughing or smiling when things got serious.

I pulled up his pants and buckled them. I don't remember if I put on his shoes. I told him, "Come on. Let's go to the store."

I don't remember if I gave him any weed, but my brother gave him forty bucks. We bought him food and things from the store for him to be good for the weekend.

I asked, "Sean, why would you give him money, man? Don't give him money. You know what he is going to do with it."

My father couldn't control himself. When he gets stuck in his habits, no one can control him. My father is a good guy. He rubbed his mother's feet. It shows you good people make bad decisions. It still hurts me till today, thinking about how addiction to drugs is a disease. That habit is sometimes so hard to break. From there, I was like, "Pops, you really got to stop doing this."

I just kept it moving.

I stopped from seeing him as much. I tried to help him hold his money one time. The program was sending me his money. The first week, he came all the way to Brooklyn to ask for that money early one Saturday morning. I didn't even know he was coming. He lost the money again.

I still tried to help him by taking him to the doctor, and one day he asked me for money.

Once he gets what he wants, he doesn't care about how he treats you. I experienced that myself. I'm not saying I am a saint. I say things nicely when I want something. My mom always told me I was good at this. Then I would go back to being an ass when I wanted. I would talk how I wanted to.

My father tried to act tough and bold. When I tried to take him to the doctor, he was telling me where the office was, he was wrong seven times, and he was yelling at me. I took him where he needed to go. When I was leaving, he said he wanted the money from me. I wanted to give him the money, but we both knew what he was going to do with it. I told him, "The money that you have should suffice."

I tried to walk away from him. He walked off and then walked back after me, crying. Ahhh, I took him home, got him whatever he wanted, and kept it moving again. I didn't realize that this pattern kept happening with my father.

My father showed me a lot about myself and my childish ways. It allowed me to grow past my own ways.

He's gotten a lot better now, and so have I.

He hasn't really been asking me for money. I keep his money for him since I'm in his life. Now, I make sure I'm there for him a few days a week. I am his home health aide right now. The reason he had a home health aide is that I made sure he had one. The insurance didn't want to approve it. I spent six weeks working on his claim for him to even get some help. I took the position over a job because I have my company, Body, Mind, and Soul BMS LLC. I have goals to work on for this world peace project and becoming financially independent. I saw it as the best thing to do for my family, even though it was a low-end budget for me. It would fill in the gaps. The real reason I did it was that the caretaker would take care of him, but he was getting weaker and weaker. The people didn't force him to exercise or book follow-up appointments.

I tried to help him as much as I could.

I helped him then, and I continue to help now.

Let me go back to the school story. I was in school. I had transferred to study Chemical Technology. There, I gained some of my biggest gifts.

I was looked after, and people really loved me. God was always taking care of me and sent the right people into my life.

This older woman in Organic Chemistry came into my life.

When I was taking Organic Chemistry, it was my first time not doing well in a class. I got As in all my classes. The professor, Dr. Nicolas, said the tests are based on homework. I did the homework and would get all the answers right, but I would not understand how I got the answers. My mind could just formulate the answers. On the test, we needed to know terminology, what primary and secondary hydrogens were, all the stuff that I could have known if I just read a page in the book. I didn't even own the textbook. Textbooks were expensive.

When I got that 55 on my test, a lot of other people failed the test as well. It was either I would get a D, withdraw, or get an A.

I bought the textbook that night. I always liked a challenge. That's the only reason I earned my Associate's Degree in Chemical Technology and graduated with an A in the class. When I read the textbook, it made so much sense I started tutoring six kids in the class. The reason it made sense to me is that a woman in my class, Sherry, gave me a book by Dr. Wayne Dyer, *Getting in the Gap*, and after reading that, I started meditating.

Everything connected in my head after I started meditating. Many connections happened, especially when I meditated after studying. I started teaching it and answering questions in the classroom. The teacher would give his praise, telling me I was so smart because I made complex things simple. He was impressed by me. I didn't even think twice. I was happy he was giving me this appreciation and focusing on the good that I was doing. That brought my passion out even more, and I got really good at school. I wanted to be a scholar like him.

When you focus on the good in someone, that is what will expand. Focus on the good in people if you want good results. Seek greatness out of people and pull it out. What we focus on expands.

He brought the goodness out of me. My family, my mother, and my sister judged me based on my past. I don't blame them. What you do affects the whole family.

I was still smoking, but it wasn't affecting my life per se. Of course, I could have done more if I didn't smoke. I am not suggesting vices because you could do a lot more when you take that nonsense out of your life and replacing it with things like practicing more meditation, working out, whatever you need to do. That was the worst thing I was doing at that point. My mom and my big sister would pick on me because of things from the past. My little sister and I didn't get along after I came back from Trinidad. She even stopped picking on me because she saw how much they would pick on me. I was working full-time hours then. I was doing so many things right. I was becoming so good at school. I was an A student and barely had time for myself. I would sleep for three or four hours, and they would still get at me. They would attack me for no reason. They would start fights, and I would stand up for myself.

I didn't let them talk down to me.

That started more fights. They weren't physical ones, but they liked to attack me. Thinking about it now, they probably saw my potential and thought, *Damn, why did he waste so much of his life?* They were probably hurt inside and upset themselves. Later on, I apologize to all of my friends and everybody for doing what I did because it wasn't even just about the crime. It is about how I disappointed everybody. How did I make everybody else look?

We stood together. Sometimes, people don't realize everything they do affects every single person around them.

One day, I was taking my little sister to the dentist on the bus. I did not know a little girl could have so much wisdom. She said, "Jay, I see how mommy and Vanessa are treating you. Why don't you just be the bigger person?"

That little girl changed my whole life with one line.

I started shutting my mouth. I started being quiet instead of fighting. Even my girl put it into perspective at that time.

She said "Jay, be happy you are alive. Your mother could have had an abortion."

Later on, I thanked my mom for not having an abortion and for having me. I hugged her tight. My mom loves me dearly. We are all fighting our own battles.

She was more into drinking. She was a party animal herself at one point in her life.

She loved me a lot. I guess I hurt them a lot.

My little sister telling me to be the bigger person helped me stop a lot of fights. I told my mom what my girlfriend said, how I could have been aborted. I found out that before my big sister was born, my mom did actually lose a child, and before me, she had lost another one.

We are all blessed to be here.

Sometimes we don't realize how precious life is.

But it is precious.

Live to seize every moment.

I seized every moment as much as I could. I became the best in all my classes. My graduating GPA was 3.83, the highest in the whole department. I remember the first time I touched a bone. I wanted to cry because I realized I could still be a doctor.

No matter all the troubles we go through in life, no matter all the challenges we face, if you just keep going and keep your head up and your shoulders back, you can have whatever you want.

Winston Churchill says, "Success is going from failure to failure with no loss of enthusiasm." It is true.

The reason I even went into anatomy class and realized I could be a doctor was because of that lady, Sherry. I was going to become a pharmacist because that is where chemistry was leading me. That is another reason you have to decide where you want to end up first, or life will dictate where you go. Then my plan was to become a pharmacist to allow me to have enough money for the life I wanted, and I would then become a doctor. Pharmacy wasn't too many years of schooling, and it was simpler. Sherry came up to me and said, "Jay, do you know you are taking all the classes to be a doctor? Don't you want to be a doctor?"

That changed my life forever as well. That's what got me on the path. That's what got me into that classroom holding that bone. That's what made me graduate with the highest honors in the department. I had a great mentor, Dr. Jay Deiner, who allowed me to research with him. I graduated with the Emerging Scholars Award in Research. I worked on a few plans. I researched and quit my job in my last year in City Tech.

I asked my mom, "Mom, can I quit my job? I don't want to have to do school over again because it's becoming a lot."

My mom always had my back. She had to sign paperwork stating that she would provide for me because I was on probation. I should have kept a job. I didn't realize how valuable it was, even if it was a few hours. As soon as I quit my job, though, I got a $2,000 grant every semester for the STEM program for doing so well in school.

I picked up research, so I even got an extra $500 for that. My mentor, Dr. Jay Deiner, started paying me from the CUNY Research Foundation.

God always takes care of you. Follow your dreams, and you will always have more than enough.

I graduated with the highest honors. I went on to study biochemistry because when I went to Hunter College, that was the major that was going to accept most of my previous credits. I thought it sounded cool, biochemistry.

The reason I always did good in school and whatever I do is because I do whatever I need to get things done.

I do whatever it takes.

If you tell me this is what I need to do, this is what I will do.

I'll talk about Hunter College next.

Human nature is to get good at whatever you do.

NEW SCHOOL, NEW EVALUATIONS

The young lady, Missy, I keep mentioning, and I went through some real experiences. She helped me overcome a lot. I was exiting a lot of trauma in my life. I wasn't the best person, and my associations were horrible. My habits overtook who I wanted to be, and it affected me greatly. It affected all of my relationships. This girl was my first girlfriend. She showed me love in her own way.

Let's start before with how the relationship even started.

I had talked about it before but let's wrap it up.

When I met her, she was already with another guy. They broke up before we started going out, but I was hooking up with her while he was cheating on her as well. She didn't even know.

Karma bit her in one shot, right?

What goes around comes around, even to me.

She gave me grace. Even in front of this one class, my homeroom for Hospitality Management in high school.

I was in the class every semester for four years. When I was missing, the kids would know, not like the other classes where they are not sure who you are and what you do.

These kids knew when I was missing, especially my teacher. When I came back from getting in trouble, Ms. Vee cried when she saw my information went to Rikers.

Ms. Vee and I had those experiences. I had coffee with her a few months ago, ten years later.

So I had come back, and all the kids were watching me, but they all loved me. They knew that we all go through challenges. This was the class where my girlfriend brought me strawberries and other food when another student let her in. She even brought it to my desk.

She would kiss me on my cheek and walk out. I hadn't been loved like that, ever. Not that I could remember, at least.

She was showing me what love is.

She would always cook for me. I got to experience her. She was the first girl I ever slept with. We were very attracted to each other, physically and mentally.

That's all we did.

Smoke, have sex, eat.

I gained that extra thirty pounds the summer after I got out of jail when I stopped smoking weed. I switched those habits to eating.

In this relationship, we were always down for each other. We saw each other practically every day. Every month was an anniversary. We really spent a lot of time together. She had to face a lot of the hurt I felt and deal with a lot of the habits I acquired.

You attract who you are.

One day, we were hanging out with three or four girls and she was talking trash to me. I told her to shut the f—up, and she did it. She allowed me to have that sense to change, she gave me grace, and she didn't run away. I realized that I was hurting this young lady, that she was not doing anything wrong, and that I had to change. I had to become better. She did not deserve this. Those things slowly made me start changing. Her mother and father were Italian and Norwegian. I'm a different color, a different race, and they accepted me into their family, even the grandfather, who lived through the time of racism and segregation. They even said that a colored kid was coming into the house when I first came over.

They accepted me. I was very respectful. I would help them with things and around the house.

As soon as I came into the house—I wouldn't even be there for five minutes—her mother would say, "Hey, Missy. Did you get Jay food yet?" She always said it right away. I could barely enter the house.

I would have dinner with them. She and I smoked every day.

That first summer, working at Nellie Bly, we learned how to work long hours. That was the summer I got three shades darker.

When we met, I helped her wean off of coke. We smoked more weed, and then we got back into Xanax. We were going down that path again. I didn't like it. After a month or two, I got off the Xanax when I got into CASES. I got off everything besides ecstasy.

When we worked at Nellie Bly, we did it a few times. We even did it one time when we went to the circus with the family. We took ecstasy, and we went outside to smoke a cigarette and were pretty obvious. They knew we were up to something, but they didn't know what it was. I was supposed to stay home because I had a curfew from the government, and we ended up hopping in a cab and going to a party. My mom was super upset.

She yelled at Missy, "Hey, if you really loved him," blah, blah, blah.

My girlfriend was crying. I told her, "You know, I'm not supposed to be going." It felt like I was holding her back from a life of fun that she wanted.

I wouldn't want that kind of fun anyway, but I didn't know at that age.

We went to college. I started putting more positive habits in my life, slowly changing more and more, having less time to smoke or do anything else of nonsense.

Everything I earned working at Buy Buy Baby those two weeks and H&M, I gave away.

I gave a little to my mom, but I would spend most of it on my girlfriend and going out to eat. I didn't even shop for a wardrobe, which I should have done.

My girlfriend even bought me an iPod one day and told me, "The reason I did not ask you was because you would never accept it." I was never accepting and never took the gifts people tried to give. I just always gave everything I had.

I was rejecting my own gifts; it started from learning not to want anything more when I was a child.

Smoking weed really kept my temper down.

When I got sentenced to five years of probation, I started back smoking pot and selling weed again with all my friends. My best friends. I had six or eight of them working with me.

I was going down that journey again. One day, her cousin gave us a chocolate with mushrooms inside, and we split it. We were scared to take it, but we took it. That was a life-changing experience. I was hanging out with my father still. He gave me the option to smack somebody over the head with a bat and get fifty or sixty grand because he knew they would have it on them.

I was thinking of doing it, but when I took the mushrooms, I realized and told myself, "You are already out of jail. You know you have to stop selling weed." I realized that I'm not here to hurt people. God didn't bring me here to hurt people. I was bound to get in trouble staying on this path.

God brought me here to help people. This was when I decided I would never hurt anybody. That's when I stopped selling weed.

I never went back to selling weed after that. I called all the guys and told them I was out and to keep whatever they had. Some of them said, "You know how long I have been waiting to hear that?"

We were already in college for a while. We were still young and going through life. Some days, we cut college and just went out. I remember one day, we went to the Statue of Liberty. She had a whole bunch of pot on her. We almost got in trouble.

A K-9 from the police started coming after us, and the cop held the dog. I guess because we were coming off the island, he didn't care to search us, or he could tell by the pull that it was not a major thing.

On the ferry going back, we saw something really funny. This lady was about to eat a chip, and this seagull went and grabbed it out of her hand with his beak right before she put it in her mouth, kicked off her face for momentum, and flew backward. The family started laughing at the woman. That was super funny.

We continued to grow together. We got stronger and stronger.

We stopped smoking again, but we kept going back and forth. Smoking was my pastime. It was hard to get away from it. I saw what jobs were like and how they sucked the life out of you.

Once I heard they wanted me to be on track to become a supervisor, I started taking up fewer responsibilities. I started not coming in. I did not want those roles. I didn't want that life. I saw the life the managers and supervisors had to live and what they had to put up with, and I didn't want to put up with it.

I learned how to work that system like I learned how to work the high school system. I would miss high school days, even months at a time, and still come in and pass the test.

They could not do anything once you have notes, and I learned how to create notes very well.

Missy and I went through a lot. For me, my problem was jealousy. She had many guys. She was my first girlfriend, and I was going through all the college experiences, seeing all these other women. I would get thoughts.

She had always promised me a threesome. Then she became more and more against it, and eventually she didn't want to do it. I could understand why, but I couldn't understand why she promised it.

On my twentieth birthday, these two beautiful girls, this Asian girl and a beautiful light-skinned black girl, saw me in lab class. I would work with two people older than me. They would allow me to lead. I would tell them exactly what we needed to do because I had read the lab and I was prepared. I was not trying to control them. I was just prepared, and I didn't want to mess up. These girls saw me take control. That was probably attractive to them.

They came up to me and said, "Oh, it's your birthday. Why don't you come back to the crib, and we will do whatever you want." I was not that confident with myself. I told them no. I could have had a threesome right there, but I said no. I was loyal.

One time I was coming out of a class. I had rushed to this class because I had so many other things to do before the class. When I got there, I didn't even eat my breakfast. At the end of class, I was sitting there, eating my breakfast, and this girl came back in. A beautiful girl, Alma, vice president of the student body, came and sat next to me.

Oh my God, she was beautiful. She started talking to me and asked me a few questions, then said in her accent, "I have been analyzing you for quite some time." This beautiful woman is telling me she's analyzing me. I was thinking, *I analyzed you quite a few times too.*

We started walking down the hall together and talking that one day. She ended up getting stopped by a professor, and she told me to wait, and I did not. I knew where it would have led, and I had my girlfriend.

I kept myself out of that way of life.

When you focus on your growth and dreams, people become attracted to you.

Then I started catching my girlfriend lying about little things, smoking cigarettes and stuff like that. The trust was not there anymore.

I was going on the straight and narrow.

I was finding purpose in my life. I wanted to get away from all the bad things that I did already. I guess she never had that realization of how badly the things we were doing were affecting us. She was okay with doing it. It was my fault. I did not always lead by example.

It is not her fault. It is usually your fault most of the time.

I didn't lead her in the right way. I kept leading her back into temptation every once in a while when it was okay for me. She was stressed with school, and she had her own stresses.

When I caught her lying, even over a cigarette, I didn't feel like I could trust her. Then when we drank, we would have bad drinking issues because I would bring up that and those things that were under the surface bothering me.

I started hanging out with my friends with her. Then we started bringing her friends around. At one point, we left all our friends.

A lot of our friends, both hers and mine, agreed with me that what she did was wrong and that she should communicate with me. Her birthday, my best friend's birthday, and even my mentor and aunt's birthdays were all on the same day. We definitely had a connection. Their birthday is 2/15, and mine was 5/12, exact opposites.

A spiritual lady told me that with our signs and the year we were born, we're actually meant to be in poverty. It was another reason I decided I didn't want to be with her.

That kind of influenced my mind.

We kept going back and forth into these bad habits. The more we tried to get away from the drugs, the more it created tension and conflicts in our relationship.

Once, we went to a wedding, and one of her cousins, a guy that was not too closely related, was all over her, talking and getting super close.

I was very jealous.

I kept thinking about all the experiences she had with other people. I didn't have those experiences. She was a flirtatious girl, and getting drunk never played a good part in anything.

I would help her mom cook. I made her aware of washing the dishes for her mother and told her to stop making her mother work so hard.

I was family-oriented. I had good morals and principles underneath. It was just that all of the other stuff, like hanging out with my father and sticking with her, that had taken over.

Her mother and father weren't doing well, but soon as I came into that house, they started doing better in their relationship because they remembered what love was. They had an example with our fresh love.

I went gun shooting with her father once. We used to go play darts with her family as well. We had good experiences. I went on a fishing trip with them. We went to a lot of weddings and family dinners together. On the first, July 4, we went out with her family. I had half a case of fireworks. I split it with my brother.

I made some of my money back by selling fireworks to some people that were there at the barbecue.

We lit up a whole bunch of fireworks, and I connected with them. Our relationship kept getting better and better.

I hung out with her cousins. Everybody loved me. I would always be there for Christmas, all the holidays. I got them more gifts than my own family. I was so into this girl's family, and she wouldn't come around my family. That's when I realized, some women pull you away from your own family and forget that your family is important to you and they need to make time for them as well. But they want you to make time for their family. I've seen it happen to my friends, and then I slowly started realizing I was doing the same thing. I could have also been too focused on her.

I helped her grandfather out. I would see this old man shaking while doing the gardening. He had two granddaughters that wouldn't take charge and do it. They would not even offer; they would say, "He doesn't want our help."

I said, "Pops, I'm going to do it tomorrow. Don't touch it."

I just went and did it. I would even clean their windows.

I brought back the morals they probably already had. They just needed the reminder.

We can all use a reminder.

She was a very good host. We were both very friendly and sanguine. We would win in beer pong. We were amazing teammates. We even played ball against boys and beat them.

We were a cool match. We had a great time.

Our relationship started shifting around the time when her grandfather died.

We were getting drunk a lot. One time we had a little fight.

Well, that was after. So let me stick with this one.

That summer, I fasted for thirty days. When I was fasting, she kept antagonizing me every day. She would say, "Hey, you want to be with other girls," because I had wanted a threesome.

I said, "Babe, I don't care about that, I care about you. If that is going to affect our relationship, I don't care about it."

I don't know if she had already talked to her ex-boyfriend or what happened.

For a few days, she kept saying that I wanted other girls. She kept pressing.

I said, "You know what? Yeah, I want other girls." And then she broke up with me for a week or two. I was fasting for the last two weeks, and those same two weeks her parents were gone, she threw parties at her house and had a wild time. The day fast ended, I rolled two blunts, and I went to her house because I knew where the keys were. I called her a whole bunch of times. She was at Mary's block party, and I think her ex was there as well.

The first hit I took of the marijuana, I realized that I was being childish and should just move on. She came back to the house, and our relationship carried on for a while. I even saw the guy's pants in the bedroom. She said, "Oh, he spilled something."

I let it go.

But my mojo and intimacy were never the same with her. We continued for a few months until my last full year of school.

I had one more semester, and I was doing well. I had just started at Hunter College. I was killing it. I was getting As, and I was the teacher's favorite student in Spanish. Biochemistry was very difficult. They say it is the hardest class in medical school. Since I wanted to be a doctor, I said if I'm going to spend all that money in medical school, I had to get an A in this class. The teacher said that people who come from my school don't do that well. I said, "Well, I had the highest honors in that school. I had the highest grades." She said that didn't matter.

I said, "Okay." She tried to put me down. It could have been a challenge or motivation. I ended up getting an A in her class and shut her up. To me, it was a challenge.

Next semester came around, and I did well again. Biology class was super difficult for some reason; the professor was super difficult. My girlfriend's grandfather had recently died, right before we started back together. He went on a trip, didn't want to use a wheelchair in the airport, and ended up taking a long walk. This pushed his body over the edge, causing renal failure. He died within a year at ninety-two years old.

We had a great relationship. He even played beer pong once. He was ninety-one years old playing beer pong. He didn't drink the beer, though. I even beat him at pool. He used to tell me about his war days. He would buy me gifts and cook special things for us. I would go with him to pick up water sometimes. I loved him dearly.

I wanted to go out with other girls when that first break up happened. After I saw her ex-boyfriend's pants and the pictures of the big party, I never wanted to be in a relationship with her again. When we drank, it revealed that I didn't trust her anymore.

Then her mom died. A month or two beforehand, her mom started to get a lot of back pain. They were moving into the house after her grandfather had died. Her father was too cheap, or they couldn't afford to fix everything and pay for the stuff to be moved downstairs. The mom was helping a lot and got sick from it. She was feeling this back pain, so she went to the chiropractor and she got her back cracked. She still felt really bad. She went for a check-up, and the doctors told her, "You have cancer."

Her mom and I had a great relationship. We danced together, and we played sports and board games together.

They threw me a whole bunch of birthday parties in their backyard. My birthday was the first birthday of the summer. My mom would make some sick, amazing barbecued chicken, all types of burgers, shrimp, chicken, turkey, and beef, with coleslaw. I would invite my brother and my friends. We had a great time, every time, every summer, for two or three summers. They bought me a boxing bag. They treated me nicely.

I was traveling home from school, and my girl called me and said, "Jay, my mom has cancer, and they said she has two to six weeks to live."

I was on the train. I just pulled my hoodie over my face and started crying. I was in love with that lady. She was such a good lady to me. At that point, I had a better relationship with her than my own mom, probably even my girl.

She was very accepting and forgiving and didn't hold grudges. She was a very understanding lady.

That was my first time crying. The next time I cried was when she actually passed away. I cried with my mom and sister when they came over to bring bread for the family.

I was strong through the whole thing for my girlfriend. I would sleep on the couch with her two to three nights to be with her and her mom. She was in pain and getting more and more brain dead, so we had to keep her on morphine. We hadn't smoked weed for like two or three weeks, and we had some left. We went to smoke outside one night. The next day she passed away.

I think it was because I was destroying my life and my chances when I was there. I think that affected a lot of things.

Every time I did drugs again, after I had stopped, somebody passed away. I went to Miami when I was working my job, and my uncle, my auntie Gulian's husband, died. Next time, while I was in Costa Rica doing ayahuasca, one of my cousins fell off the train and died. He was doing art, taking pictures while subway surfing on top of the car.

When her mom was passing away and going through this trauma, I was in school. I had to make up all my test because I missed a few days to be there. I missed two tests for the funeral. I told the professors ahead of time that something serious is going on. They let me take the makeup tests.

I still graduated with high grades. I graduated college with a 3.79. That semester affected me a lot though, or else I would have graduated with a 3.90.

We were going back into drugs and getting high. I remember when I was fifteen, when my friend's father died, I got into smoking weed even more. I did not know how to sympathize with the situation, so I tried to numb or pacify my feelings with drugs.

Misery loves company.

That got me into doing worse things, and putting me back down that path. I saw it happening again. I was scared. I separated from my girl at that point. She would go to the bar and get super drunk but I didn't go. When she came over, I told her to stop being the way she was acting. I could not even put it into words. I was upset with her, and she knew I was upset because she wanted to go out with people. I did not want to go to the bar. I knew it was not good.

That's when our relationship started drifting because I wasn't going to accept her doing the wrong things. She wanted to. It was my fault as well because that's what I taught her when we had tough times. She came over to the apartment after getting drunk with her cousins, and I don't even know why we started fighting. She ran to my roof and was acting like she was going to jump off. She and her mom were best friends. It was so hurtful to see. We were having fights too. I remember we did a toga party and that was my first time ever touching her. I was blackout drunk. I chugged a can of beer. They lifted me up into a handstand over an ice bucket, dunking my head until I couldn't take it anymore. When I got up, they gave me spiked punch. I can't even remember what was happening when we argued. I grabbed her arm and she had a mark there.

We weren't good together anymore. We were too toxic with each other at that point.

That day she was going to jump off the roof, I knew she was hurt by her mother passing away. I grabbed her and said, "Are you crazy?" I pulled her back downstairs. She was like, "Let me go home." I couldn't trust her to go home. I wrapped my legs around her and held her down until she went to sleep.

She continued to fool around, get drunk, and go to parties. I think she was at a party with her father, who had broken his arm on a deck before, and she ended up doing the same thing.

We continued for a little while longer. Our relationship kept drifting apart. I had signed up for a summer class and graduated from EMT school. We were going through all this stuff while I was in school, taking 16.5 credits and taking an EMT course. In school, I was overloaded and still dealt with this relationship. When I finished that semester, I knew I was going to get a job because I wanted to make money again. That summer, that first month, I got a job right away. I wanted a job, and I got it.

We started drifting more apart because I had to stop drugs and smoking to become an EMT.

I wanted to join FDNY to be able to help my mom, which wouldn't have even helped, thinking about it now. I was so strong in my emotions for wanting to help my mom and then this girl. It took so much of my life, so much of my energy, and I saw how her mom pass away. I didn't want my mom to have that life, and I wanted to be able to help her. I was tired of wasting my life.

When she had broken her arm, she broke up with me. When she broke up with me, her world was smashed. Her mom died, and she had spent two years going to court reporting school. Then she broke her arm. And she was just passing 225 words a minute.

She was all messed up in the head.

She didn't want to pick up court reporting jobs when she had the chance. She went to work at a bar with her uncle and aunt, the owners. She started working and got into the bar lifestyle. Being a bartender was not good for her. I distanced myself, and she broke up with me. I felt really bad when she broke up with me. She even said something along the lines of wanting me to go experience other women. I didn't want to. It broke my heart that she was trying to break up with me in order for me to go do that. In the first two weeks, I had the chance with one woman, but I messed up because I was stupid and naïve. I was not listening to her opening the door for me to have my way.

If I listened, I could have had what I wanted.

That happened with multiple girls. The second time, I had this girl naked, but my mojo wouldn't work because I had only ever been with one girl. This girl I was with was beautiful. I didn't even expect her to be so beautiful. We met in the gym at school, and she was super smart and super intelligent, and I had just started going to a gym for the first time in a while. I went a few times before. This time, I was transitioning from smoking pot, and I used the gym to change the habit to something positive. I was going to school for a summer class, working a job four days a week, and working out.

To rid old habits, replace them with new ones.

I started seeing this girl. When we went out on a second or third date already, she told me no, she didn't want to do it. I was feeling myself, and her pants were down, and everything was right in front of me. She was on all four saying, "No, no, no," but everything felt like, "Yes, yes, yes." Again, the connection was still growing, and I was only with one person. I pulled up my pants. She thought I was being a gentleman. She buttoned my shirt and tied my shoelaces. I didn't call her when I got home, so she thought I was like every other guy. I didn't even know there were rules to this. I had never been with other women before. In the first two weeks, I got with two other women, but I never completed it. I didn't sleep with a woman for a whole year after.

Let me just end this relationship stuff.

Her cousin called me because when I would call her, she wouldn't answer. I stopped calling her after a while. I guess it was because I was supposed to go experience life. Then two weeks before my sister's wedding, her cousin called me and said, "Jay, I didn't know you affected this girl's life so much. She's out here, screaming in bars and kissing dudes." He told me she was acting like Trina.

I called her, and I said, "Yo, what's going on with you? Your cousin is telling me all these things. What's going on?"

I said, "Don't let anyone mistreat you. You are a queen. You were the captain of your ball team. Do what you got to do."

She asked me, "Am I still invited to the wedding? Your mother invited me. Can I come?"

I told her, "No, you can't keep going back and forth. You can't play with my emotions like this. I'm human." When I said that, that's when the relationship was over.

Next, I'm going to talk about my journey into Kappa Sigma, and the end of my relationship with her. She always knew I was there for her, but I'll talk about that in the next chapter.

After that summer, I really transitioned away from Missy. I was instilling a lot of positivity into my life, like the gym. The gym helped me stop smoking and allowed me to sleep because I was really hurt when we broke up.

I did very well in school. Then I went on to my last semester at Hunter College. I was in the gym, and this guy came up to me and offered me the chance to join a fraternity. He told me they were the number one fraternity in the nation and all these good things. He said, "There's no hazing," and talked about the network. When I heard networking, I said, "That's what's up." And no hazing? Even better. It's about raising gentlemen, community service, things like that. I went to one of the street school fairs. Everyone was representing their organizations. There were tables for different clubs, fundraisers, and movements.

I saw this new fraternity about to start up.

I was looking at them and talking to them. Then I saw one of my friends that used to play basketball, where we used to smoke pot. He was more of an acquaintance. He was the younger generation. I smoked while they played ball. I used to chill there to think and get ready to make the most money.

He was really good at basketball for a young kid. I saw that he was in the fraternity that the kid had offered me to join. I said, "Hey, tell me why I should join this."

He said, "We are number one. Why would I go for number three instead of going for number one?"

That was it. He told me it was a good thing. I joined.

We had to go through a process to be a part of their fraternity. This started eating up my time. While I was joining, I was in college classes, volunteering at a hospital, and I was an EMT on the weekends. I believe I started Toastmasters later. I had a lot going on for me. I was working out five days a week.

Now I was joining a fraternity, and it took work. This potential brother and I were the busiest outside the fraternity, and we put in the most effort within the fraternity. The other kids were only taking classes. We worked, I volunteered, and he worked more hours than I did.

We were working on a team project, and I realized I had a lot of leadership skills. I took what other people said they wanted to do, and I made it into one project within the organization. It was for a fundraising project, and it turned out to be fun. The delta class was exciting and fun.

I joined that fraternity and got really into it. I was finishing up my classes, working out, and sleeping four hours a night. On Sundays, I would sleep eight hours during the day because I was working the overnight shift Saturday, and I'd be exhausted. I literally couldn't get up after I worked the overnight shift and not sleeping very much the whole week.

My meditation practice was very high at that time. At this point, I hadn't been with my ex-girlfriend for a while.

I started talking to this girl named Ema in my biochemistry class. I decided I was going to pick up a girl, so I went to talk to her. She said that she just wants a friend. I had just gotten out of a serious relationship and was looking for a friend as well—and thinking on the naughty side too.

We hung out a few times. Once, we had a private studying session in the library, and she was on top of me. We were making out, and the security guard, who knew me, walked in and then walked out, closing the door.

She said, "If you say you're my boyfriend, we can go further."

All my friends said I should have said, "Yeah, I'm your boyfriend…for the night," in your head. I didn't think that way. I was a very honest guy. I said no. I have to think about that. I told you, I just came out of a serious relationship.

I didn't get nookie that day.

I was still talking to my ex because one of her friends called me and said, "Jay, this kid that she is with is not treating her right." I had seen a picture on Facebook. I didn't like the picture.

He had his hand in her shirt in the picture on Facebook. To me, it was degrading.

I found out he was being an a—hole and he wasn't being nice. He was taking advantage of her, and I think he had crashed her car a few times. It's crazy how I didn't like anyone doing that to her, but I was blind for all the times I did wrong things to her. I never disrespected her physically, aside from that one time I touched her arm. I treated her respectfully in public after high school.

I called him up, and he never wanted to speak to me.

One day, I called Missy. "Hey, I want to come by and see you. I know you work in the restaurant."

She said, "Okay, come by. But you got to behave, though." The last time we actually hung out was the time when I had blacked out drinking from the devil springs punch and the handstand chug.

I went. We chatted, and you could see that she was in love with me. Her heart was still with me. That was done. I wasn't going back. She already posted pictures with other guys. We went down the wrong path, and you can't play with my emotions. I didn't want a life like that. Because you think I'm feeling some type of way, you are going to do other stuff with other people and tell me how it's going to go. That wasn't right.

She loved me. She was a good girl. She gave me whatever I ordered. She served me. She was admiring me, looked up at me, and wiped off my pin. I had my delta pin on until I joined the fraternity.

I went there to tell her again, "You were the captain of your ball team. You are a leader. Do not let anyone mess with you."

I told her, "That's not going to work out. You don't deserve that. You deserve someone to treat you like a queen."

We were chatting for a while. I left a $20 tip, paid for the food, and dipped. My heart was still there. I was so focused on what I was doing, and I didn't want to go back to my old ways. I was scared I would go back to my old ways very easily with her.

Remember, I had taken the EMT course. The instructor's name was Oscar. He was in front of the whole class, and his wife called. He answered her FaceTime call and said, "Hey, this is the guy I told you I am adopting," and he turned his camera toward me. I was laughing. He was a cool guy. I loved him. We had some good times, and he taught me a lot. I did transport for three to six months. They said, after you do transport for that time, you can work to get into 911, through the hospitals.

I did that, then I went to talk to Oscar because he worked at Long Island College Hospital, right across from the school I went to on State Street. He told me, "Jay, you can write a recommendation letter. I will sign it."

I wrote it up, and when I went and sat with the supervisor, he said, "What? Oscar has been here for years. He's never written anyone a recommendation letter."

My interview process was the question "What was your favorite subject in college?"

I said history because in college, I realized that Boston was where the people stood up against Great Britain. I never liked Boston because of the Red Sox (we were Yankees fans), but when I saw Boston was the one to stand up, I didn't mind the Red Sox anymore. I started liking Boston. They took the stand for our freedom.

What is funny is, as I write this, tomorrow is July 4, and I'm talking about this chapter of my life.

I was on this journey. I had gotten a better-paying job now. The hospital was closing down. I should have kept both jobs, but I was so excited, I quit the other one. I got a good number of hours at LICH.

I graduated with all As, and one A– in biophysical chemistry, though I was supposed to get an A. I don't know how she graded, but I let it go.

My sister was married now. I had given her $700, all the money I had at that point, as a gift. I borrowed money from my mom to give them more money, and then I paid my mom back.

My sister actually paid for my ticket to go to Trinidad because I was unsure if I was going to go. She bought my ticket and said, "You are going."

We went and saw my grandma and my family. It was Christmas. It was my first Christmas away from my ex. I felt so hurt. I felt like, "Damn, I should have had her here."

My ego was high. I took lessons from my father. He said you can't go back to a girl who was with other guys. That's one of the biggest reasons I didn't go back out with her.

She started going out with this older guy. He was thirty-two, and she was twenty-three. He ended up engaging her a few months later but influenced her to get back on coke, a friend called and told me.

I tried to break it up a few times because I didn't like what he was doing. He was taking advantage of a young girl, influencing her with cocaine. He was a grown man. I was ready to beat him up. One time, I texted her when I was working EMS, right after I came back from Trini.

I'm going to talk about Trini in a second. I just want to finish up with her.

I ended up texting her. I said, "Hey you tired of being with a loser? You want to be with a real champion?"

He called me from her number, and he started getting crazy.

He said, "You want to fight me?"

I said, "Yeah, I'm ready."

He said, "Meet me here."

I said, "I will be there in three minutes."

I made it to the bar in three minutes and went to the back to check the whole bar. He wasn't even there.

This cocaine story came up again, one of her friend's reached out, and we got on the phone again. I don't even remember how these things happened anymore. When we talked, he was acting tough again. He said, "Why don't you come meet me?"

I said, "Yo, bro. You are a little b—. Last time I came, you were not even there. You fronted. I am not coming to meet you. If you want to fight, you come meet me."

I gave him my address and the bell.

"Ring the bell, I will come downstairs, and we can fight the fair way. Come upstairs, you're a dead man."

He never came. That was it. I went back to the bar a few times. I saw him once. I wanted to go back out with her at that point in my life.

We kept it moving. I was working and studying for my MCAT.

That's where I was; that's the interim of my life.

Where is the bottom?

Let me tell you about the hospital. It closed down. Production was slow. This happened on the day of my brother's birthday, the same day my grandma died.

I'm going back to when we went to Trinidad. That Christmas was the first time all the grandkids were there together in over fifteen years.

My mom was there before us. We were all excited to be flying because we flew with Roderick, a family friend. Roderick made it a good time, and everyone else as well. I hadn't been on a plane in ten years. Hameraj, my aunt's husband, walked me into the house and started giving me a tour. He brought me into the back and showed me the nine queen-size beds and the rest of the house. I was there when it was just a concrete frame. I killed snakes over there. I put the poison around the house. That was where we used to farm.

Then he showed me the laundry room. He showed me everything. When I first entered the door of the house, before Hameraj showed me all the bedrooms, I heard my grandma and my mom say, "Oh, look. He is not even looking over here. He bustin' style."

After the tour, I went and kissed everybody, then I went to kiss my mother and my grandma. I said, "I wasn't busting style. They were showing me around."

I held my grandma's hand.

When I held her hand, she looked into my eyes, and it was like she could look into my soul. She said, "I know you've been doing really good up there for the past ten years."

I was like, *Damn, Grandma. For the past five, I've been doing really good, but for the first five, Grandma, I did horrible.* I thought that in my head. I didn't say that. The way she looked in my eyes gave me the strength. I felt like I should be dropping down and doing push-ups. That was the strength she gave me. I became very serious. I did not laugh until I became an EMT and worked with my friend Derrick.

Thank God I loosened up and learned to connect with him.

Wow. My grandma gave me strength with a look.

My aunt gave me purity and no worries. When I was at her funeral, these emotions flowed through me, giving me these freeing thoughts, putting me at ease.

Older people put a lot of love into me, a lot of wisdom.

The other day, I saw my sister, Vanessa, in my head when I woke up. She said, "Our life is changing for the better. We will have all of our dreams."

We hung out. We had a really good time. During that whole trip, the one thing that stuck with me the most was the feeling my grandma instilled in me. We were there for my cousin's wedding. We helped him like crazy. We did all of the decorations, set up the food, arranged chairs and tables—the back-breaking activities. Then the party began. My blue suit was too tight, so I couldn't breathe in it. I had this beautiful girl named Sarah dance with me, and I couldn't even have fun with her due to the restrictions of my suit. She liked me, but she probably thought I was a lame dude. She died recently, I was sad to hear.

We did so much work for that wedding. I felt like I did the most work. We always feel like we do the most work, but I know I put in a lot of work. At one point, I was sitting there with my grandma at the wedding. She was in my arms, and I fell asleep. That's how tired I was. I think we had a few drinks. I'm not sure. I wasn't drinking much at that time. It took one beer to knock me out. I was stopping everything. I had to stop so many things.

I had a great time. We went to the beach, and I could have definitely slept with Mily, one of our family friend's daughters. She tried to grab my crotch one time. The next time, she was in a beach room by herself. She always tried to play me and mess around with me. I almost threw her into the ocean. She was really trying to push my buttons and see what kind of guy I was. I may have had sex with her, even though she was younger, but it would have been wrong.

I hadn't slept with a girl since my ex. I didn't speak to any girls after the three initial girls. I was still trying to get comfortable with girls. I went to a party later on. It was a fraternity brother's birthday, and I went. The young girls were being so lame. You had to play so many games to get in their pants. I was like, "Oh no. This is annoying."

So I called this older lady I was talking to, and I said, "Are you going to teach me dancing?" I was going to learn salsa with a sixty-year-old woman.

I went over there in my mom's car. She wanted a bottle of wine. I bought a bottle of Hennessy as well. I should have drank the wine or nothing at all. I didn't even get to enjoy the time. She was teaching me how to dance, and then she started getting freaky. Then everything started happening super fast and ended just as fast. She wanted me to go again. I fell asleep and woke up and left. She wanted me to come over a few more times. I felt so scared. I was like, what the hell? I hadn't had sex in so long. I was doing it with a sixty-year-old woman. She was attractive and very fit. So many negative thoughts were going through my head. I should have just practiced more with her and had a good time and learned how to dance, but I was young and naive. It would have been a good experience.

I was still taking the practice MCATs, and we had found out my grandma was sick. As soon as we left Trinidad, we found out she had lupus. Then they set up the will.

My uncle was upset about how the will was set up; everybody was fighting. My grandma was sick. She was by my auntie Nadia's. She could not be in her own home. My cousin had gone and told my grandma everything that was going on and wrote a big long letter to read to her. I think it made my grandma even sicker. They were fighting in the hospital, triggering my grandma to have a heart attack. My brother and I were planning to go down. That weekend we were going, she died.

She had another heart attack because they were fighting again. She didn't recover from that one. We were going down to see her. Everything happens for a reason. We had already booked our tickets, but we got our money back.

We had good times. She was a good lady, and she showed me a lot of love. A hardworking, amazing woman, Zorida Mustapha.

EXPLORING LIFE

I got another transport job. I had two or three transport jobs. I went to Conclave for Kappa Sigma in New Orleans. I was doing a few alumni events. I went to the bar with them and had a cigar. I was exploring life.

When I went to Conclave, I had just started RCA, an ambulance company. I was going to work at First Response, but this paperwork went through faster. I went to RCA, and while driving, I was acting cool for this girl who was working with me. I ended up accidentally jumping the curb and scaring this woman with her kid. I jumped back off the curb. She got super terrified and notified the company. It was my fault. I didn't hurt anybody, but it was my fault.

The day I was hopping on the plane for my trip, the guy at RCA called me. I already got the days off, so I was like, "Why is he calling me?"

I answered and he said, "Hey, don't come back to work."

I was like, "What?"

He said they received a report about me driving recklessly. I did not deny it. He told me, "Come back and bring your uniforms."

I said, "Okay, that's cool." I didn't like it anyway. I had to go all the way to Staten Island.

I didn't even want that job that much. I ended up going to Far Rockaway at one point to work.

I worked at First Response. I did that for four months. I was still doing the volunteer service at New York-Presbyterian. I was studying for the MCAT again, which was the week after my grandma passed, and I failed. I got a 23 or 24. I could have done very well. I was getting 29 and 30s on the practice tests. That week before the test, instead of focusing and grinding for the last week, I ended up playing basketball, having fun with this girl named Jennifer.

Basketball was something my ex-girl and I used to play. Guess I used it as an escape so I would have an excuse if I did not do well.

After I slept with the older lady, I felt so disgusted with myself that I went and slept with Ema. I told her whatever I had to tell her. I said, "Yeah, you can be my girlfriend." We went out on our first date, and then I brought her back to my home and closed the deal.

I stayed with Ema. I made her my girlfriend at this point. I was doing First Response when Christmastime came around. Since I volunteered in the hospital so many times, I went twice to the EMT office at NewYork-Presbyterian. I dropped off my resume and all my EMT certifications to the director's office, the head of the EMS department. No response. I didn't drop it off again. I was a little discouraged. Then I had a patient that worked EMS in the hospital. She was in the internal medicine room, where I was taking care of patients.

We told each other our story. We connected. She told me she worked EMS for the hospital as well and that I should apply again. She gave me the encouragement to apply again. I applied again for the third time.

A week later, Lori, one of the head EMS supervisors, called me, and she said, "Hey, I hear you have been applying, and I want to get some reference numbers from you so I can speak to somebody that could refer you. Can I speak to your current manager or supervisor?"

I said that she could, though I didn't build the greatest relationship with them yet. I had just started working there. I said, "Well, I volunteer in the hospital. You could talk to my supervisor there since she is in your organization. You can get her feedback."

She agreed. I gave her the name and number. Then within five or ten minutes, she called me back and said, "Well, the lady can't stop talking about you. I want to interview you over the phone right now."

We did a phone interview. Then all I had to do was the human resources interview, which was just a formality. I did that and got the job, earning $20 an hour. They told me I had to stop volunteering.

I started my career. That was Christmastime.

They gave me those two weeks. I had to work on Christmas. I was super happy to get the job. I was doing well again on my practice test, and I was happy about this job. I took the Kaplan course this time. Right before the test, I was so excited about this job and making extra money, I started doing childish things, like drinking again and doing all this extra stuff. It threw me off track, and I did poorly on the test again.

That was it. I had to take the course one more time, and Kaplan was going to give me a free course. There was a new test; it changed from a four-hour test to a seven-and-a-half hour one. I quit First Response with only a week's notice. They didn't like that.

I did not care. I did not like First Response because the lady supervisor and I were getting into it. She did not want to give us lunch breaks, tried to overwork us, and tried to tell us what to do when we were out there in the field. People sent us on dangerous calls. I did not like how most transport companies worked; they didn't do the right thing. I ended up leaving that job. I started this new job. I was in Toastmasters, and I believe at this point another one of my fraternity brothers was the president. That gave me more reason to join.

DELVING DEEPER

I went on to the journey of being an EMT at New York-Presbyterian. It was a great job.

I was making as much money as my sister, who is a teacher, with my four-month certificate. That messed up my head. What really had my brain going was that I spent four years studying biochemistry and four months becoming an EMT. At the same hospital, if I used my credentials, I would get more money as an EMT, than apply with my biochemistry degree for research. It showed me having a college education doesn't guarantee you a better-paying job. I was making the same as my brother, my mom, everybody. Yet my mom contributed more to the family than I did. I realized that it was not enough. I did not realize that right away. It was enough for me at that point because I really got to enjoy my life. My mother has always been a blessing, allowing us to be free and experience life. I got the job, and I started giving her $300 a month. I continued to do what I needed to do. That excitement of having this new job and this new income, I ended up failing the MCAT the second time, studying for it again, then went for another six months doing well on the practice tests. I don't know how, but I stopped focusing again.

I didn't feel like doing it anymore. I realized while being an EMT, I didn't want to serve the way doctors had to serve. I was sitting in the library of Hunter College, studying. I realized I didn't want to sit there for the next four years. There was so much I had to do. I didn't want to sit anymore. This was about three years ago now. In one year, I would have finished medical school with $250,000 in debt. It wasn't even about the debt. The question was, was I going to do this for the next four years of my life when I had such big visions and dreams? Was this the only way to achieve my purpose?

Stand in your vision.

I didn't think this was going to cut it because my dreams had changed. I wasn't a five-year-old boy anymore; I was twenty-six. It's obscene to ask a five-year-old kid what they want to be. Yes, we need direction, and that did give me purpose. It's a good thing, but we have to think: What kind of lifestyle do we want to live? What is going to get us there, that would give us purpose, and give us motivation? The question is a little off. We should explore our gifts and talents and see how we can use those to get what we want. At the same time, what we choose to do should support the lifestyle we want. My passion is the life I build myself, not necessarily exactly what I do.

I would choose to be happy with anything I do.

I was sitting there to take the MCAT again. When I was studying, I didn't like being there. I was watching how doctors had to serve. The EMTs would do all the grunt work, bring the patient to the doctors, and deal with some crazy situations. I went through all spectrums of society's classes. I went to the project buildings within New York with cockroaches crawling on people's beds, right on the wall, all over. The guy had a broken nose, the bone had created a gash in his nose, and he didn't want to go to the doctor. We had to get a supervisor on-site because that was against medical advice. Then there's the other spectrum, where I was in a six-million-dollar condominium with gold fixtures, literally gold fixtures. It's a one-bedroom with a magnificent view. They were complaining about a headache and wanted the ambulance.

I was exposed to a lot: gunshots, people shot in their butt, people stabbed walking around, babies being born, heart attacks, families watching as you do chest compressions on their loved ones, EDPs (emotionally disturbed patients), screams, people cursing us, and the obscene scenes and scents.

I saw a lot of different lifestyles. I saw places I wanted to be and places I didn't want to be. I saw people, choices, and things that showed me what I didn't want to do anymore. It made me think about what gave them that lifestyle.

Your choices decide your lifestyle.

I kept doing EMS for a while at the hospital. I did it for two and a half years. I really grew up while there. My coworker JS showed me how to not get taken advantage of. Even when I volunteered in the hospital, this lady, Beverly, taught me some amazing lessons. She said, "Jay, you can't help everyone. You can't just pick them up, even though they ask for help. Let them help themselves."

I was very thankful to have learned that lesson because I would have definitely broken my back working. I was trying to help everybody. She was like, "No, let them help themselves because if you don't let them do it now, when they go home, they won't be able to take care of themselves."

She told me that we want them to grow stronger here because the more we do for them, the less they're going to do, and they're not going to get stronger. They are only going to lose their capabilities. These patients have to do more or do as much as they can, so they can keep growing instead of weakening them by doing everything and making them handicap and invalid. She did not say it in that dramatic effect, but that's what I understood. I was working with JS, and now I was getting paid for this job, and I almost went back to doing everything for people.

I saw him do things that I wouldn't have done, like pick up people on a chair when not recommended. We saved these people's lives. One guy we saved already had low systolic pressure, maybe fifty. We are supposed to put them in the Trendelenburg position on a scoop stretcher and take them downstairs, but we flipped him onto the chair. We did it very rapidly as soon as we got to the stretcher. It worked out perfectly, and he came right back. Who knows what would've happened if we had done it exactly by protocol. It may have taken longer and been more detrimental.

That was a bad example. Let's talk about some regular stuff. This guy fell down a few stairs, and he wanted us to pick him up on a scoop. He was in a basement. We'd have to go upstairs. You could tell he wasn't hurt. We checked out his PMS (pulse, motor, and sensory) on all his extremities, and he was fine. He was moving around before we even got there. He wanted us to pick him up and carry him, I guess because his ego was hurt. He fell in front of the woman that he was with.

We didn't pick him up. JS looked at me later because he knew I was concerned about why he didn't pick him up.

JS had been to war; he was an Army veteran. He said, "Jay, my friends got their limbs blown off, okay? I've seen that happen right in front of me. These people are complaining about back pain and belly pains and all this nonsense."

He told me, "These kids are younger than us. They want us to pick them up. No. If they can walk, we're going to help them walk. We will assist them. If it's really bad, of course I'm going to help them. Jay, you see how I move. I'm not going to pick up everybody. I'm not going to break my back." That gave me perspective. It helped me save myself a lot of trouble.

I will assist those that are willing and able. I am not going to pick up everyone.

I was learning a lot from him. He taught me first aid stuff I was supposed to learn in EMS class, but they only teach you the fundamentals. They don't teach you real applications, even though they have some hands-on modules for us to do. It's not like dealing with a real human being that's in pain and agony, and his bones are popping out or his limbs are hanging, and you see the bone protruding. It is not the same thing. He taught me a lot of that, he would say it is time for Sunday class, and we only worked on Thursday and Friday together. He made fun of me.

Good guy. We had a decent relationship. I was childish. He said that I raised his blood pressure a lot. When I stopped working with him, he said, "I finally stopped taking my blood pressure medication."

I started Toastmasters a little more vigorously. I was practicing for my speeches outside the van, and one time I got in trouble because I went up on this high ledge. I was sitting there, meditating, and the security guard said I could not sit there. JS was laughing because the guard was kicking me off.

I was trying to get into meditation. I was hanging out with Geneva, the monk, a lot. She was preparing me to do classes and teach more. We were doing classes at colleges. I had two or three big sessions at Hunter College, teaching meditation and meditative practices with about eight monks. I then taught lessons every other Tuesday for a full year, on Forty-Third Street in midtown Manhattan, where I would make salads and fruits for everybody and bring it to eat. It was a small, moderate turnout. I was treating it casually, but it should have been packed.

Casualness will kill you. Seize every day, every opportunity, and do your best. Serve as many people as you can, the best that you can.

That was my gift, then I would teach them lessons. Lessons that I put in my first book that I published, *Abundance a Journey from Anxiety and Depression.*

Toastmasters put a lot of light inside of me because everything we wrote about and the speeches we had to listen to were full of positivity. It took away more time for hanging out with people that were not good associations. I had to force more positivity within myself. I liked the curriculum. It was a beautiful experience. I enjoyed it very much.

In EMS, I saw how all these things were working. I was learning the field. I see all the doctors were forced to treat these patients a certain way. I shadowed a few doctors at one point. They don't have much time with the patients, so they can't really figure out all the nitty-gritty details. They have to prescribe certain medications and treatments because they have to follow the Hippocratic oath and do what's best for the patients based on all these guidelines and protocols. To me, we're treating the symptom. We're not really healing people, and some of these things are probably making them even sicker.

You have to treat the whole and not the symptom, or something else will pop up.

I feel we can heal ourselves. I saw meditation starting to heal me. I saw good nutrition was healing people as well. When I was in the ambulance, what was the number one cause of most people's illnesses? What is the number one cause of all disease in the world? It is stress. Stress leads to drug addiction, heart attacks, diabetes, obesity, bad eating, poor mental health, and more.

That is the number one cause, and I realized we could really heal ourselves. I started teaching meditation more. Meditation is an active training of the mind, helping train your mind to think differently and approach situations appropriately. It helps reduce our overwhelming thoughts, which stop us from changing our habits. The overwhelming thoughts make us anxious, and we do things to suppress that feeling instead of learning to relax the mind. When we relax the mind, we learn to control our thoughts. Our thoughts manifest our lives. The more we can control our thoughts, the more we can control our life. Better than the word control is to come to peace with our thoughts and with ourselves, creating compassion, grace, and clarity.

I started getting into that more because I felt that was what I should be spreading. When I saw my little sister, she was a little chubby. I wanted to teach her how to heal and connect with herself, but I did not realize how chubby I was.

It is easier to see other people. I did not see myself and how I could work on myself.

I said, "Maybe she'll listen to me if I become a nutritional therapist and personal trainer." When I read a book by my friend Kinja Dixon, *Universal Talk Laws*, he mentioned things I have always done, but I never realized, such as when you have a comfortable position and you're making good money, you should still build while you're there. You should be working toward that next step of life. It is analogous to what we say in our organization, "Dig your well before you're thirsty." Realizing a job would never retire my mom and allow me to enjoy life the way I wanted to. I had to think bigger.

I was working on that heavily. I became a nutritional therapist and personal trainer while I was working in the EMS position.

I started working out more, becoming very fit. Within the first two or three months of Toastmasters, they had assigned me to the audit committee chairman. I was speaking in front of three hundred people. I was exploring life. In my first month of EMS, I was in the newspaper because I was a diligent worker. They called us for a job. The call was in Brooklyn, and I was in Manhattan. I flew down there, nice, smooth, efficient, and safe. I was the first EMT on scene because I didn't wait and stall. The guy, according to the newspaper, fell off the Brooklyn Bridge; he was still alive in our care. Eventually, he passed away at Brooklyn Hospital.

I learned nutritional therapy and personal training to be able to teach my sister, but it ended up affecting my life greatly. I started my first company, Body, Mind, and Soul. I had one client. I didn't see it being too lucrative. I saw it as side money. I thought, "Oh, this is a waste of time." People want to work out, and they think that's enough. If you are stressed at work or anywhere, you are going to develop high cortisol levels. You're going to eat badly. I know from experience; I used to be an emotional eater. I realize all these things are affecting people. They have to do everything; they can't just work out. They have to meditate or take care of the mind. Meditation can be prayer or exercise. It is staying focused, clearing your mind, journaling, using artistic outlets, chanting, practicing gratitude, and so much more. People have to take care of their nutrition and eat right. Most people think that if they work out, they can eat whatever. The thing is that diet is 70 percent of the workout. If you work your abs, you become hungrier. They are feeling the pain in their stomach. It's not really hunger, but it's pain, and the pain they usually associate within the stomach is hunger. It was counterintuitive, but if they were not going to listen to the whole program, I didn't want to train them.

When doing anything, you need to do the whole thing for optimal results.

I didn't know how to grow that business, so I did not focus on it too much.

I was stuck in the safe paycheck mindset, waiting every two weeks to get that hit. I played safe and did not work my brain.

Being in speaking and with all the light filling up inside of me, I realized I didn't want to be a doctor. I was wasting my time. This was not where I wanted to go. I didn't want to do this for the next four years. It was a childhood dream. It was time to wake up and do something different.

When I was twenty-one, and in Kappa Sigma during college, Jon, my best friend in my delta class, asked me, "Jay, can I try this on you? I just became a life coach."

I said okay. He said, "What's your purpose in life?"

He gave me a whole bunch of criteria from Jack Canfield. I used the criteria, and I wrote my purpose out, but I was going to be a doctor. I went down the path of being a doctor, but my vision grew just from writing that purpose, subconsciously.

If you have unlimited potential, you have all the resources in the world because we're all one. The only thing separating you from having everything in the world and access to everything is asking for what you want and enrolling others in your vision. I believed it.

My vision grew because I saw how I can help more people. What I wanted to work toward was world peace. I planned to work to end suffering, making sure everyone has food, water, shelter, and clothing, furthering that to holistic healthcare and education. I want to inspire the young and those who have given up on themselves.

Down the path, I was hitting goals. I was working hard. I realized one of my biggest goals was charity, and charity starts at home. I was going to make sure my mom and my family were good and that they lived a great life. If I'm worried about money, how am I supposed to really help people?

That's why I have to become abundant in my mindset. I have to do things that let me live abundantly. I have to create income where I don't have to sacrifice all my time.

People say rich people are greedy, materialistic, and only care about themselves. People say that the rich get richer as the poor get poorer. These are limiting, debilitating beliefs.

For the rich to make a lot of money, that means they had to help a lot of people, for one. They had to create jobs or serve people in some way to do whatever they did to create wealth.

Two, the more you have, the more people you can help.

If you believe the rich are greedy, you are never going to become rich. Break all these stigmas about rich and poor. The rich get richer because of their habits, not because they have money, only. I'm not saying money doesn't help. But the poor stay poor because of their habits. The poor people have poor habits, so they continue to live a poor life. If you change your habits to rich people's habits, you'll become rich. It's all about your habits. Our whole life is based on habits. We are creatures of habit. We have to decide what we want in life. We all have twenty-four hours.

That is what I was seeing and realizing. I had to be very careful of who I was listening to and what I was doing. At that point, I asked myself, "What is going to make me money so I can fund my dreams?" I became a real estate agent while I was an EMT. I did that for about six months and closed about two rentals. I got jipped. I worked on a team, and the guy shorted me on money. Then I went into sales and switched over. Before I had switched over to sales, I had gone to San Francisco with my sister, which threw me off the rental game a bit. That was when the guy shorted me on the rentals, which made me want to get out of rentals and change from being part of a team. I had no incentive to stay. I was doing the work and making a few dollars. I had to learn and sacrifice in the beginning to acquire new skills, but I did not realize that was what was happening. I wanted results quicker; I was used to an instant paycheck, doing work for two weeks and getting paid. It is a different mentality. I know I was not doing as much work as I could because I was so drained. When you don't do the work, you get affected more, you get tired quicker.

I realized the more I worked, the more I hit my goals and did things that I said I was going to do. The more success I had, I realized that I had to stay on track, or I was putting myself down more. The law of inertia states a body in motion stays in motion. Regardless, I was overworking myself. Some weeks, I would sleep two or three hours for two to three days in a row.

I went to San Francisco with my little sister because she graduated as the valedictorian of her high school. Well, of course, I wanted to build my relationship with my little sister. It was also that my mom had to work and my other sister was going to Europe. My little sister wasn't going anywhere. In my family, we didn't really give too much encouragement and appreciation. When I graduated with the highest honors in the department, I didn't get much praise for that. In families, they are not taught to give you good reinforcement for the good things you do. That is most people. It's not just my family. They highlight all the negative things you do. People get attention for the negative. That's why we do more negative things. If we got more attention for the positive, like my professors gave me, I would have probably done more positive things and done better. That's why we have to take every chance we get and praise people for the good they do.

My sister and I had fun in San Francisco for ten days. We explored. The first day when we walked into the Japanese tea garden, I felt the abundance of life. How fortunate are we? There are so many possibilities out there. We have to do whatever it takes to make something happen for us. There are so many ways to live an extraordinary life. We have to go out there and make it happen.

We were bonding a bit, but then her boyfriend broke up with her on the fourth or fifth day through text while we were cruising down Highway One in this amazing Mustang drop-top. I paid an extra $600 to give her that experience. She enjoyed it for a bit. We went to the top of the Twin Peaks, then we drove all the way down to LA from San Francisco on Highway One. We went to the wharf and had fish and whatever she wanted. We got chocolates and souvenirs. I didn't know San Francisco was cold. It's in California. I thought it would be warm.

I had to buy a jacket while I was there, but I got a souvenir out of it. We had a good time; we enjoyed ourselves. We ate diverse food and went and met her family. We went to the Warner Brothers Studios because she's into film and acting. We built that relationship as much as we could, though that breakup affected her and affected our trip. She started acting b—hy while we were driving down to LA, out of nowhere. I didn't know what happened because we were having a good time the first four days. I said, "Yo, what's wrong with you? Why are you acting like this? You better stop this."

She stopped, but she was still upset. She didn't tell me anything. Now we went to Starbucks and got something to eat. We were leaving Starbucks, and I was depressed walking around with my sister. She was being super mean. I looked up, and this lady looked up at me and smiled. She just warmed my heart and made me feel better.

That's what we get to do. We get to affect people by being good people and sharing good, positive love around us, smiling and simply saying hi to one another. Humans are meant to be social creatures.

We get to spread positive energy. She made my day better. My sister didn't want to get out of the car or go to any of the trails. I told her to come on, and she listened. We took some pictures together, and we had a little bit of fun. I love my little sister. She's so beautiful. When we reached over to another peak, where I was going to stop, near the halfway point or three-fifths of the way down the trail, I said, "Let's stop and eat."

When we got there, she burst out crying and told me her boy-friend broke up with her.

I wanted to call the kid up and yell at him. What would that do anyway? Trying to tell him to be with my sister sounded stupid to me. I didn't even know what to do. If I was smart enough, I would have called him and had an educational talk with him. Why would he break up with the girl while she's on a trip?

When we sat down, she didn't want to eat. She was upset. I said, "Jesse, love is worth it. I really enjoyed having my first girlfriend. It was a great experience. We grew together. We learned a lot together."

You attract who you are.

I could see that with Veni, my current girlfriend. I told Jesse you attract who you are. That's why I was working on myself. You want to be very careful about what you do. I told her, "You have to take the time for yourself and focus on you. Guys will always be there. If he is the right guy, he will come back into your life. Don't be scared to love or go on dates, but focus on you, focus on your life. Get what you want, and you'll find a guy in your field in the things you're already doing."

That advice worked, and I found Veni after I started working on myself. I went back to work after two weeks and didn't like it very much. It was a great job. I loved the people I worked with. I was working overnights for a while now. After the first year of the hospital, I went into overnights because I was going to try to make more money and go work an additional job. I never got another job. I chose the real estate thing. I guess that's how I treated it, like a thing to just try instead of realizing the opportunity and taking it seriously. Not doing the things you know you should be doing takes a toll on you. I was getting upset that I was not doing as much as I could do in real estate. The team dynamic affected me initially with the money mishap. It didn't have to be an excuse, though. I could have made it a reason why.

Eventually, I switched over and went into sales because I knew there was more money involved in it.

The guys in the ambulance said, "Jay, you need a break. Not a break, more like you need to go do some drugs or something. Get out of here."

I had already gone to Miami that year. I partied like crazy. I didn't even have a good time. I was still living like a child. I could have had a better time. I had this beautiful white girl speaking to me the whole time, but I got so drunk, I couldn't even drive well. We had to take an Uber and then go back and get the car.

I was upset because I was in such a scarcity mindset that I didn't want to spend my money to pay to have Uber take me to the actual spot. I had a great time. I knew the girl was into me.

I was wasted, and I let that be my excuse. I was drinking too much and sniffed coke for the first time. I tried it once before but never felt it or had the experience of the high. I put it in a joint the first time.

My uncle Pooran died that weekend. I feel subconsciously that my family pays for the choices I make.

Now this next trip I went on, I went to Costa Rica. I saw an advertisement for Costa Rica on Facebook, and I remembered my friend Jon and Moore going there. The post said a plant-based medicine retreat. I'm thinking this was a vegan retreat where we were going to eat healthy, do yoga, and stuff like that.

A guy called me up from the retreat and told me if I knew about ayahuasca. I didn't know anything about ayahuasca, but I have heard of DMT before, and it was related. My coworkers were telling me I should go and take some drugs. These were guys I looked up to because they worked hard and stayed with the company for so long. They were a bit more mature than I was. I decided to do it. I went there, and I had an amazing experience. It was a great time. I met Danny, Amy, and a whole bunch of cool people like Jules, Kev, Jim, and his girl and her friend. I remember the lady that ran this ceremony and her daughter, who was super cute.

They were such beautiful, awesome people. It was a great experience. I would not recommend someone do it, but I didn't regret that I did it. I had a good time. I knew the girl, Jules, was pressing on me and wanted me after the first trip we had, and I didn't want it. I was pure for the last month because that's what they recommended. I was not having sex or anything like that. I was eating clean and being as pure as possible.

When I came back, I had two different women in that same month. When you want something enough, you attract it. When you want something bad enough and focus with strong intention, you will achieve it. On that trip, we were doing yoga every day and eating healthy, good foods, all vegan and vegetarian. The two nights of the ayahuasca ceremony, we dressed up in white, and we went into this place within their own little backyard jungle, where they built a large canopy where the ceremony would be held. We had our own flat mattresses. It was dark outside; only the lights of the fire glowed. Everyone was in their own separate bed, trees surrounding us. The silence filled the air, and the anxiety grew. We all went up one by one and drank this green liquid, and there it began.

The first night, they recommended to us to stick with a mantra. The first night, I stuck with it; the second night, I didn't. On the first night, I realized, as I was lying back on this bed they had for us, that I was feeling like a prince. I felt I had to work on my sacral area more. I was neglecting that. I wasn't nurturing that as much as I could.

Then I felt like I wanted to throw up and poop at the same time. I went to the bathroom, but nothing would come out. I was in the middle of the jungle area. I was crouching down, feeling pain in my stomach. I built back up my strength. I was feeling like Vin Diesel all dressed up in white. I was a bit more muscular at that time. I was working out. I was feeling myself, and I got up. I felt ready for anything. I was having visions of a panther coming at me, and I was ready for it. Then the thought came into my head, as I was ready to fight, so what if you could fight? What is that going to do? I was humbled by the thought: what is fighting really going to do for me?

I relaxed. When I was lying on that bed, before I got up, the thought of being a motivational speaker came into my head. I saw that you could have anything you wanted and be anything you put your mind to. You just have to follow through. That's what came into my head. My mantra was love, and I stuck with love all night. What came into my head was, *Jay, anything you do, just do it.*

You could become anything you want. Just follow through and do it.

It was a powerful feeling. It was telling me, *Jay, anything you want.* If you want to become a motivational speaker, what does it take? You just have to do it. We went back to the main cabin. We ate what they had, some granola mix. Oh my God, it was such a beautiful resort, and I had a really good time. Then we went to sleep, woke up early, did yoga, ate breakfast, and went through all the purity rituals again. With this ceremony, you have to perform it twice. Kev didn't want to do it the second time. He was bugging out the first night because he had many epiphanies and all these high thoughts.

I went to do it for the second night.

I didn't want to do it either. After having the first night, I was good. I know what I can do. The second time, I didn't stick with my mantra. I completely forgot it. I witnessed a lot of wickedness, a lot of bad thoughts. It was a lot of bad dreams, not dreams but hallucinations. I was having really bad stomach pain. The first night, I sat in the back. This time, I was sitting in the front, next to the girl named Jules because she came, hugged, and cuddled with me the night before. I know she wanted more, but I pushed her off and asked her to go to her room. On the second night, she was bugging like crazy. Her arms were rapidly swinging around; her arms were wings, like she's going to propel off the bed on the wooden canopy.

I got up and took a walk. I couldn't go back to my bed because of her, so they put me back in the back. Every time I went in the back, I felt the forest was taking me and sucking me in. I visualized bugs and nature consuming me. I couldn't stay back there. I ended up going to the bathroom. I was going through a whirlwind. Every time I closed my eyes, I would see patterns, sick patterns, multicolored, geometry intertwining. I feel an urge to throw up, and then I would need to use the toilet. I was back and forth in this constant whirlwind. I would go to throw up, and the patterns would begin as my eyes were closed. Then it shifted to stomach pain. I was holding my stomach, and my head was spinning. This went on for what felt like twenty to thirty rounds. A guy came and knocked on the door.

His name was Dave, but he reminded me of my sister-in-law's brother. He said, "You okay?"

I told him, "Yeah, I'm all right." I had kind of started coming back to reality.

You can get stuck doing drugs. I thought, damn, my family gave me this amazing life, and I might get stuck doing this. I might get stuck on this trip. I started to feel guilty. Then I was understanding what had happened to Trisha, my father's roommate, who was stuck on the trip. She kept going back and doing the same cycle. I said to myself, "I do not want to live this life. I can't do this. I don't want to do this to my family. I don't want to get high anymore. I don't want to do drugs."

I kept going through a cycle, observing that I didn't want to get high anymore. I hoped I wasn't wasting my family's time, and I was sorry if I had.

I got up, and I made it out eventually. Dave helped me out, not physically, but he kept checking on me. He looked scary at first, and the host of the ceremony came, she looked really scary, like a witch or a demon. I went back to the canopy, but I couldn't go there because this girl had her arms swinging around, and I didn't want to sit in the back. I went by the fire. I saw this lady, this beautiful girl. I liked her, but she had a boyfriend. I wasn't going to press her, but she was very flirtatious. I did not pursue her because she had a man, but I looked at her, and in front of the fire, she grew old in front of me. I could spend the rest of my life with someone until we grew old, was the thought that entered my mind. It was more of an analogy for me to understand that when I found a girl, that I could spend the rest of my life with her and grow old.

I started taking care of the fire and throwing firewood in there to keep the fire burning. I was beating myself up, feeling like a failure. I had this clear path to become a doctor and was now trying to do this real estate thing. The keyword was "trying."

Why don't you just follow through on one thing?

Now you're wasting all this time when all this time you could have been doing other stuff. I feel people think as a motivational speaker, you are there to motivate them to live their dream, but you are not going out there to do what you need to do and live your dreams. People are going to judge you, regardless. I realized that I did not want to be a doctor, but at the same time, not following through with something made me feel like a failure. I was experiencing that. I was feeling that in a major way, and it was taking a toll on me.

I kept putting the wood on the fire.

This analogy came into my head that the fire represented life. I saw I needed to add more wood to the fire. Keep doing more, keep going. The fire is life; just keep your life going.

Keep doing more.

Keep adding wood to the fire. Add more things into your life. Do what you got to do. Just keep going, Jay; you will live an amazing life.

I had a great ayahuasca trip. That was the end of it.

I woke up out of it when we were all hanging out. I went out with the crew on our last day at the retreat, and I ran the beach by myself. We ate and saw monkeys all over, took public transportation, and got to bond. It was cool. I shared the room with them. They left that night.

The next day, I ran down to the zip lines about a mile away. I hung out with the girl Anna.

When I went back to the hostel for two days, I wrote a lot in my journal, a little bit about this experience and how I was going to create world peace. I wrote about the projects I would work on and about throwing retreats and other things I would do to progress in life and serve.

When I opened the door of the hostel, I could see a whole land of a tropical forest, and I had a hammock to swing in and watch the scenery. I was working out every day. I was feeling good, and the girl Anna came home, and she didn't bring her boyfriend. I don't know if it was really her boyfriend. I ended up going out for tacos with her. I introduced her to Danny.

She said something, and she thought I got offended. I could have gone to her room when she went in. I ended up not going in because I was going to go smoke if I went in there with her. I knew I would have ended up doing more with her. When I was leaving the next morning, I wanted to end things with her the right way. I already had my stuff in front, and the lady was coming to call me in a little bit. I brought a cup of tea to Anna, and I said, "Let's sit outside and talk before I leave."

I met Danny before when I brought my bags up front. He called me up, and that was why I went to the front. After tea with Anna, I said bye to her, we made out, and she was so cute. I would have had fun experiencing her. She reminded me of my first girlfriend. She was super pretty, super beautiful, and short, you know, five feet two, fun-sized.

I came back to New York, and I was in a high state of depression. I didn't feel well. I was upset that I was going back to work. I wanted to quit my job.

I didn't know how to get out of it. I wrote my resignation letter a few months later. In November, I became more depressed and tried to numb my mind. I remember when shares of Ethereum were $8. Kev and Danny told me I should put money into it. I would have gotten $200,000 from that.

I was contemplating making this transition in my life. Was I doing the right thing? I was not making the phone calls that I need to do to build my business. I felt like I was asking people for handouts. I didn't really want to ask people for stuff. Oh! Ask, believe, receive. Asking and enrolling others in your vision is important, especially if you have a bigger plan for life. "You should have just asked," I would hear. That's what I'm doing in this business. I am asking. "Ask, believe, receive" (*The Secret*).

I felt awkward doing it, though. It was not something I was used to doing. I am used to doing stuff on my own and doing what I was told. I was comfortable doing for others instead of asking for what I wanted.

John Maxwell says that if you have big dreams, you have to work with others. If you work by yourself, you will only be small potatoes. Small potatoes are good, but they do not last long or go as far. If you have big dreams, you have to work with others. Another thing he says is that by yourself, you can go fast, but with others, you can go further.

I was grateful for what I have, of course. I was grateful, but at the same time, why not build something more?

As I was in this transition, I knew I had to get out of my job. It was a dead end for me. I didn't want to be there. I didn't want to be a doctor, so why am I an EMT? I worked overnight, so I was in the darkness. This is right before I bought the car.

I was traveling back and forth from work at night.

At work, I would numb myself with Facebook, Instagram, and other media platforms. When I was home, I would close all my curtains and live in the darkness as well. It was wintertime. It was getting dark early. I would use pornography to knock myself out. I'd get up to eat and lay back down. It was a cycle I was going through. I stopped meditating. I stopped listening to motivation. I stopped working out. I was in this big slump for two weeks.

Then this bad thought came into my head. I had lived a good life. I never thought I would think this way. The voice said, "If life is so bad, why don't you jump out the f—ing window? Jump out. Open the window and just jump out. The window is right there."

Wow, I didn't believe I could think like that. I got up off the bed. I shook it off, and I started getting back into my routine. I started getting serious about life again. I switched over my real estate license to doing sales in Brooklyn. I closed my first deal within two weeks with my friend. I closed my first offer and still had to go through the closing, but I had already gotten acceptance from a co-op building. That would bring me $3,000 to $5,000 right there, and that was within two weeks of me deciding to go that route. Now, I was starting to make phone calls. I was going to work, being rigorous. I wrote my resignation letter in February. My supervisor had given me all my days off before February so I could go on a self-development journey.

There was a lot of transition on this journey for me. I decided to go to a personal development workshop, which was recommended to me by Charlie, who got second or third place in an international speech contest at the Toastmasters contest. I was there with him through one of the district finals. During those two weeks of depression, I broke up with all the girls. I was still with Ema and the married woman.

I wasted a lot of girls' time. I was wasting my time too. When I came home from Costa Rica, I slept with this older woman who was thirty-seven, and I slept with a twenty-two-year-old. I decided I didn't want to hurt girls and waste my time or money anymore. The next month, I signed up for an introductory course to the personal development journey.

GIVING IS RECEIVING

I had to slow down and think about how to move forward. It was in my nature to automatically think about school. I felt like if I was going to go out into the world and do so many great things, I wanted to start with my family first. I decided to start with my dad and see what I could do. This was a year or so before real estate and Costa Rica. When I went to his house, there were drug dealers there. There were kids with guns in their backs. You couldn't see it visibly, but I could tell.

They were right by the entrance of his apartment as if they were guarding the door from the inside. I came in and said, "What's going on, Pops?" We talked a little bit.

I told them, "Get out of here. This is my father's house." I kicked out Jihad, another dude that was bringing trash into my dad's house. He's a big hoarder. He would steal things, pick through garbage, and keep it in my father's house. When I cleaned it up, there were eight bags of garbage.

Three weeks later, I came back, and the gangsters were in the house again. I kicked them out. I said, "Pops, what are you doing? You told me you didn't want them in here, that you want them out. That's why I kicked them out in the first place. Now they're going to look at me like I'm the bad guy. Then we're going to end up fighting. I'm not coming here to deal with this nonsense. I'm not coming here to lose my life over something like this."

He said, "Oh, we won't do it again. I won't let them in again." Then Trisha told me how they were beating her up when she didn't let them in the house. That kept happening more and more. I feel Trisha was taking drugs from them and owed them as well.

One day I went, and there were even more gangsters in the house. I wasn't going to get involved anymore because I knew something was going to happen if I kept doing it. I told my father to come down the block and took him out to eat. While we were eating, I realized how skinny he looked. I said, "Pops, you look like death."

It was depressing to see my father. He weighed 108 or 110 pounds as a 5'10" man. When I told him he looked like death, he said, "Jay, you don't even know what's going on."

I said, "What's going on?"

He said, "At night, like twenty of them come and raid the house. We sit down quietly while they bag up their crack, like a crack house. They were all bagging up their drugs."

I said, "Okay, well, if we call the cops, I don't want you to be there. So we can't call the cops."

I told him to go by his son. "They won't want you in the house, but you can go. He is not going to kick you out. On Thanksgiving, show up at his house and tell him you can't go home."

He didn't listen; he didn't go. Later, at his program, he told someone what was going on. Looking back, this may have been the best thing because he would be out of harm's way. They called the cops. His program ended up sending him to Brooklyn, where we live. My sister rented him a hotel room. My brother knew what was going on, but his wife didn't want to let my father stay with them. She didn't want the gangsters to follow my dad to where she lived because she felt it was unsafe for her kids, which would have never happened with God's blessings. She didn't understand the dynamics.

We couldn't let him stay with us. That was my mom's place, and my mom would have gone by her boyfriend's for Pops, but I didn't want to inconvenience my mom. My mom wouldn't want to stay at the house with my father there. She was willing to stay somewhere else, the giving woman she is.

The hotel room my sister booked wasn't too far from where we lived. My brother and I drove down there that night. I hadn't smoked in almost a year, but I had a nice piece of bud at home that I had found in my hallway. I went and got it for him, rolled it up, and left it with him. We gave him some cigarettes too. He said he didn't have his medication and couldn't stay there for too long without his medicine, which was in the house. Looking back now, we could have refilled his prescriptions.

I thought, "Damn, this guy is setting us up." Thank God for my sister. My sister doesn't care; she puts her money down for her family anytime. She is such a beautiful girl. What a giving, faithful woman.

My brother was driving me home and said, "Let's go in the morning." Then he said, "Nah, let's go right now."

I agreed. He said, "First, let's go get something to eat. I'm hungry." He had just left work. We went to Vegas Diner. My brother is not, I wouldn't say, cheap, but whatever. I've never really seen my brother spring for the bill so quickly. He offered to pay and paid.

All I could picture was me and my brother going into that house and having to smash some heads, beating some people up, and going at it. My adrenaline got high for a second but then cooled off because I was with my brother. I was down for whatever. I didn't have a plan. I knew I'd figured something out. When we got there, the cops had just left, somebody said. Some of the gangsters got arrested, and the others got away. I guess the program may have told the police. Trisha was there. All the drug dealers had left.

I got my father's pills. We went back to Brooklyn. The next day was my little sister's birthday. We were going to Mystery Night, an escape room event.

We didn't know what to do with my father. I said, "Pops, if you go back home, you know those gangsters. They might come back. I don't feel safe with you going there."

When he came over the next day, my mom said, "You let some gangsters take over your house."

It was demeaning, but at the same time, empowering. That's my father. You know what I mean? I didn't want to hear that. I had to find a new location for my dad. We didn't have a place for him to stay. We didn't want him to go back home and get harassed by these gangsters. I ended up taking him to a shelter.

I found a shelter, and I called them up. I took him and walked him in. Remember, he was an old guy with a cane and could barely walk; he couldn't even hold his own bag. I brought a garbage bag full of his clothes inside, and they told me I couldn't go any further. They let me go through the metal detectors, but they didn't want me to go downstairs, where the occupants stay. Then I said, "Well, he can't carry his bag. Somebody's going to have to carry his bags down. Will you allow me to carry it down, and then I'll leave?"

They said it was fine. All of a sudden, I didn't feel good about the situation. I was like, "Nah, my father can't stay here." It was coming down to crunch time, and I had to get to my sister's birthday party. I'm very family-oriented and timely as well. I do not like to miss things involving my family. I said, "Pops, you can't stay here. I'm taking you home."

I took him home. I never realized how big this was. Going to help my father took a toll on my life. Thinking of it now, I was resilient to drama. I went to the mystery room and, somehow, cracked open a lock that allowed us to escape. My brother opened the door.

Then we had this Haitian guy, Max, stay there at my father's place. He didn't smoke crack. He didn't do drugs; he only smoked pot. He worked at UPS in the mornings. He really helped my father out. He was with my father for about two months. I had just gotten the job at NewYork-Presbyterian. I was working there for a little bit. Then in February, Max went to visit his family in Miami, Florida. This was before I went there. I stayed with Daddy for those two weeks to maintain the household. When I went there to my father's, our pastime was smoking. I ended up smoking for the first time in two years.

I didn't smoke a lot. I smoked a few hits.

That night, I went into the bathroom to think and looked at myself in the mirror. I had just failed the MCAT again. Well, I didn't fail it. But I didn't score as high as I wanted to. I could have still gone to study osteopathic medicine, to be honest, or a low medical school in the US or one of the best Caribbean schools. At the same time, I preferred to go to an osteopathic school because it was more holistic medicine.

I looked in the mirror, and I felt this surge of energy flowing through me. My hands were grasping the sink as I was leaning over it, looking into my eyes in the mirror. "Jay, you can do anything you put your mind to." I felt a strong sense of belief in myself.

I went back outside to chill with my father. We smoked again.

I started smoking every once in a while, going deeper on a more philosophical level. I started hanging out with my father more, and I started staying there frequently. I would sleep there three or four nights a week. The other nights, I would go back to Brooklyn two or three nights a week. I was still giving my mom the $300 a month, helping as much as I could. I was staying with my father because I was trying to get him back to health mentally, and it was easier for me to sleep there and go to work. I know he was happy to see me there. I was there till about March or April, and I hadn't slept with any women the whole time.

Max, the Haitian man, said, "I'm going to think you are gay. I have not seen you with any women these past few months."

My focus was not on women. I was still studying for the MCAT, which I didn't really want to do, and a few other things, like Toastmasters, working out, and figuring out my future. I wasn't really thinking on that wavelength.

Max had gotten slashed in his face a few days before, and I was upset. He had a big slash on his face. He was putting vitamin E on it to heal. He was riding up over the bridge, and these three gangsters stopped him. He pulled his chain off his bike and fought them off. He didn't even know he got slashed in the face until he got to work. He had a massive cut and was bleeding. His adrenaline was so high. Max could have killed the kids, but he let them go, not knowing that he had that slash in the face. If he had known, he would have killed them.

They knew he was there with me and my father. I didn't know if it was the kids around the neighborhood.

I said, "I want you to come outside with me." I took him and my father out, and I bought them coffee from the deli and went to get myself a Dunkin Donuts coffee. When we were walking out, Max said, "Nice color," to this girl, and she did not respond to him. He and my father were sitting down.

They said that she must be a cop. The girl was a white girl with a nice dress on, a short Spartan-like gold dress. She was by herself with no one around her.

I got up, took my drink, and said I would be back.

I went to sit next to the girl. I started talking as she was turned away from me. I said, "I hope I'm not bothering you," because I was talking to her for a while, and she was not engaging, trying to answer me but not answering me at the same time.

She started laughing at something I said. I can't remember what. Then I said, "Oh, at least I'm not doing anything wrong. At least you are laughing." Then she turned, and we started talking. I found out it was her birthday.

I don't know how this happened, but I said, "Hey, you want to go up the block to my father's place?" She had a bottle of champagne.

I said, "Let me get some strawberries right across the street." I bought the strawberries, and we took it back to the place. We drank her bottle together; well, she drank most of it. We started making out, then she said, "I have a boyfriend, and I can't really have sex, but I can do other stuff."

That was that.

When we walked back up the block, I could have gotten her number, but I didn't think of that. I bought her a bottle because she had drunk her birthday bottle with me. I think it was a bottle of Moët. She kind of pressured me into buying her a better bottle, but it was all good. I didn't care. I had just gotten what I wanted right there on the spot.

That's the start of my journey with women. My father told me, "I saw thirteen different women in my life. How could you only see one?"

Many guys influence you in the numbers game, breeding guys into dogs and hurting others.

So at this point, I had three women.

I felt like I *needed* to have a girl. They say that when you have a girl, all the girls follow you. I said, "All right. I'll go get a girl."

I knew Ema. I started going out with her with the wrong intentions, I am not going to lie. I was working out like crazy. I was getting my body fit. I was pretty muscular at that time. I was still into meditation and things of that nature. No more gangsters were coming to my father's house when we were around. If we weren't around, sometimes they would go knock on the door. But when Max and I were around, everyone knew they couldn't come in.

I started bringing girls back to my father's house. I picked up random girls on the street. I came out of the gym once and met this girl who wasn't all that, but we had a really good time. I had picked up a few girls quickly. I had my girlfriend but wanted more.

One day, I walked out of work and went to the frozen yogurt spot to buy a smoothie, and an Italian girl was in there. She had a nice dress on. We started talking, and I learned she was going to a concert. I walked her down the block. She ate her ice cream while I drank my smoothie, then we parted. That next weekend, I invited her over. She came back to the house. I could have brought her right into the house, but I wanted to treat her like a lady. When she came in, I only had my towel on. I said, "Hey, just wait here," and went to get dressed. She had come to see me in Harlem, and she lived in Queens, that was a trek.

I took her outside, and we walked and talked. We heard music playing in the park on Manhattan Avenue. We walked down into the park. There was a private barbecue. I went and sat near the old ladies. I started chatting with them. I said, "This is how you get in. Chat with the old ladies, sit down with them. They won't bother you."

They are always welcoming. We started dancing a little bit. I felt awkward, and I could tell she felt way more awkward than I did. She was nervous. You could tell she was a freak, not wanting to come off as a freak. I said, "You don't want to eat anything here?" She said no. We walked up the stairs out of the park. There was a nice area where we started dancing by ourselves, on our own exclusive platform. We could still hear the music. I took her to a Tavern and bought a little bit of food and walked back. I bought her something to drink because I knew she liked to drink. She didn't really drink much. I think she took one drink. Then we went back to my room.

She came back another time and came right back to the room. She didn't want to keep doing that. One day, I was talking to her when I just came out of the gym. She said, "Can we go for coffee or something first?"

The same thing was happening with my actual girlfriend. I was treating my girlfriend the same way. I would just tell her to come to the house. She made me get out of the house and take her out, but she was my girlfriend, so it was cool.

I told the Italian girl, "Let me think about it. I don't really want to do all of that. If you want to come by, come by." I could have had her come by, but she wanted to get coffee. I guess she was trying to gain back her self-esteem. People feel insecure sometimes.

I saw this girl looking at me when I came out of the gym, but I was still talking to the Italian girl. I hung up the phone, but the girl I saw had disappeared. Before I hopped on the train, I decided to walk around a little bit. So I walked around, and I saw her. She was looking cute. I walked right toward her, like a bull. Ironically, I was on the block of the Bull in the Financial District, right outside of a gym.

I was walking down that block, and you could see she was stuck like a deer in headlights. She was intimidated. I went up to her.

I said, "Hey, how are you doing?" We started chatting. She told me she was looking for a frozen yogurt spot. The place she was in front of didn't have it. Funny, right? The girl I was just on the phone with was from the frozen yogurt place. How ironic life is.

I said, "I know a place. It's a ten-minute walk from here."

She said, "I thought this place would have it, but they didn't. Where is the other place?"

I said, "We could walk together. I'll take you."

We walked and talked. Then we sat on a bench together. We talked for a little bit as we enjoyed the frozen yogurt. Instead of sitting right next to her on the bench, I sat on the other side of the barrier so she would be further away. I looked at her as we talked. I could tell she was attracted to me; the chemistry was building. Then I showed her some self-defense moves. I said, "Oh, let me walk you home."

She told me where she lived. I said, "Do you want to come by my place for dinner? We have food at the house that I cooked." I didn't cook it. I said I did. I don't think we really even had food. She said sure, thinking I really wanted to feed her.

I took her back to the crib, and that was it. She stayed the night. We messed around a whole bunch. She told me she was looking for a husband. She was about thirty-six. I was twenty-four or twenty-five. I felt bad for what I was doing with her. I did like her, but it just kept happening.

We would meet up often. I still had my other girlfriend and was hooking up with this girl. She would drive over sometimes. We were up all night. One night, we literally didn't sleep; the attraction was strong. I had work at eight o'clock in the morning. She had to drive me to work. I showered, and then it happened again. While I was at the gym, she would wait for me. She would take me back to the house. When I wanted to break up with her, I felt really bad. I did like her, but I knew she wanted a future and kids and to get married. I wasn't willing to give her that. I cried a little bit when I was breaking up with her.

I said, "I care about you, but this is not going to work out. I don't want those things." She was upset. We still ended up continuing to meet up a few more times.

Sometimes it is just not the right time.

We went on a trip together, a four-hour drive up to Watkins Glen. Apparently, my girlfriend didn't have Facebook, yet she saw the pictures with me in them that the girl posted on Facebook. I told her that she was my cousin.

She said, "Oh, okay," and just went with it. I could tell she was hurt. I felt bad for that too.

Then I hung out with some other girls. I met this amazing girl when I started doing real estate, Amora, a Saudi Arabian girl. She had a royal passport, and I could have gone to Saudi Arabia and become royalty.

I messed that up too. I really liked her. How did I meet her? I was on the bus to my real estate class and was on the phone with my girlfriend. I had already worked seventy hours of EMS that week. I was super tired, lying down on two seats. I looked over and saw this girl, looking cute. I hung up with my girlfriend and went to chat with this girl.

She was pissed off. I was like, "Yo, what's wrong with you?" She told me all the stuff that was going on and that it was not me. She was frustrated with school and tired. I stayed on an extra stop to get her number. I had to walk back a few blocks, but it was no problem. I got the number.

Sometimes you have to go out of your normal routine to get results, not saying I was going after the right results.

One day I went by my uncle's on a Friday night. We drank a little bit. I called up the girl from the bus, and we texted back and forth. She said she couldn't hang out that weekend. She had a test that she was studying for. Somehow, she still met up with me that night. I had my uncle drop me off. We had a drink and hung out a little bit on Seventy-Third Street near Second Avenue. I did not know she lived a few blocks away. I chose that area because I had work in the morning. I walked her home. She was telling me she was a virgin. I saw the way she looked at this black guy as if she knew about sex. She looked like a freak too. She was being nice and trying to be innocent.

I knew something about school buses: you can pop open the back door, and they're always unlocked. I popped the back door open, and I led her inside. We started making out, and I started moving forward. She was like, "No, no," but wasn't stopping me.

I said, "Okay." I stopped and dropped her at home.

I went back home and went to work the next day. I started to really like this girl. The next time, we went to a comedy club. We had a drink before we got to the comedy club because we had an hour and a half to spare. Before we even made it in the comedy club, I was already smacked off of that one super-strong drink. It messed me up.

Once we got inside, she went to use the bathroom as the show was starting. She came back and started talking to me.

"There's no mirror, and I can't see myself." She was talking loudly.

The comedian got upset. He started talking to her, saying, "Yo, why are you being so rude and disrespectful?" and pointing this out in front of the whole room. She was a little loud, but damn, chill. I said, "Hey, watch your mouth. Watch how you are talking to the young lady. The only reason she is even speaking is because you guys don't have a mirror in the bathroom." I told him to relax himself.

That turned her on like crazy. I didn't mean for that; I was doing that out of respect. I didn't do it to look good.

Later on, she said, "Can I come back with you to Brooklyn?" So we headed back to my place. We switched cabs the first time because the first cab driver kicked us out. We got into another cab. That's the cab she threw up in. The first cab just didn't like her. He kicked us out after a while, and she smacked him in the face. I told her, "Yo, chill." He wanted to fight. I said, "Stay in your car, bro." He drove off, and we got into the next cab.

I brought her back to my house, and I thought she had thrown up on my bed, but she didn't. When I thought she threw up, she was like, "I could just buy you new sheets." She was acting like a little brat.

We got up in the morning and did what I thought we were going to do the night before. Then we went to breakfast at Fuel with my sister and her boyfriend. Amora was looking old that morning. Her gray hair was showing, but she was only thirty-two. I think she was older than my sister, so my sister was feeling a little weird about that.

Later, I invited her out for Mother's Day. It was the same day as my birthday, but it was more of a Mother's Day celebration. She read one of my sister's texts that asked, "Why are you bringing her?" and felt super offended. So she didn't want to come. She took me out to a nice restaurant for my birthday.

At the same time, I was finishing up with my real estate class. I went to my little sister's graduation. I had told my little sister we could go somewhere to celebrate since she was her school's valedictorian.

Here, I started to realize even with all these women, I was still feeling lonely, with no one to come with me to my sister's graduation. It was for the best. I did not have someone to do life with at that point.

We said we would go to San Francisco and Los Angeles because she wanted to get into acting and the film industry. I knew my friend had a place in San Francisco and that I could stay there for free. I gave her $400. She told me next time I went; it would be free. When we got out there, we went to visit her aunt in LA.

I was still on a journey and still trying to be there for my father ever so often. That was getting tiring because his negativity kept growing. My negativity was growing as well, as I think about it. The more people I hurt, the more I was feeling hurt and depressed, but I was so distracted, I never realized it.

I was working super hard, doing real estate while working as an EMT. I was wasting time when I was with most of the girls. With Amora, I was really building the real estate business. I was going on so many appointments, taking pictures of properties. I was really building it.

It wasn't profitable for me at first, though. It probably would have been profitable down the line, but I did not wait long enough.

I was supposed to go out with Amora one day, but I had met this other girl the day before. I had already broken up with Ema as soon as I met Amora. I did not intentionally do it; it just happened.

I met up with the new girl instead of going out with Amora. On the date, apparently, I called Amora by accident, and she heard me talking and flirting with this girl. I had just said something nice to her.

And then I saw the phone, and I was like, "Ah, man!"

When I said that, she was like, "Are you supposed to be somewhere else?"

I said, "No."

We went and hung out at the Tavern. It didn't really go any further. Amora and I were still hanging out after that, but she didn't really like me as much. One time, I got drunk and threw up in the garbage can in her room. She was into me. She could take control and be a little freak. That time, I had gone to my friend Derrick's birthday party at Don Coqui. She looked amazing, I should have spent some time with her before going to the party.

We ended up breaking up when I went to San Francisco with my little sister. She was going to Saudi Arabia, and she really wanted me to come, but I already had plans with my little sister. So I couldn't go. That added fuel to the breakup of that relationship. She never wanted to talk to me again.

The point is, I initially slowed down to help my father. Slowing down, I was able to think bigger because in the first few parts of my journey, I never made time to think; I just did.

I got to sow my royal oats. It made me more confident with women. After my first girlfriend, the one I was with for four years, I was a little insecure.

Hurt people hurt people. My insecurities allowed me to justify doing things I knew weren't right. It helped me build up my ego, not my security. I had a good time. It was cool, but I did not want to continue doing that. I ended up breaking up with the married woman. I broke up with all the women at the same time.

If you really look, I just spoke about women for a whole chapter, which was equivalent to two years of my life with women. Most men do not become successful until their forties because they are always chasing women. Focus on you and building your future. I rather focus on one woman so I do not get distracted. It became a habit or an addiction, chasing women and going after sex. Stay focused on the real results you want in life. Everything else will follow. Every one of them you are with, you give a piece of your heart and mind. You give them your time and energy, and you will never get that back.

What I had learned while with my father was that I like rap. I got into rapping a bit. I was working on a nonprofit project in my head. I figured out what I wanted to do. I didn't figure out exactly how to do it, but those ideas were swirling in my head.

When I was smoking with my father, it was the best. That's when I would get the most philosophical thoughts. They say the blessings come from the Father. Father, as in Jesus or God. Blessings flowed through my mind as I sat and smoked with my father. I was seeing how I could help the world and do things better. I already had these thoughts, but they kept coming into my head, and they were becoming clearer.

Sometimes, I smoked to help me figure out what I had to do next in my life, but I started abusing it. I had all these recordings. Every time I would smoke, I would record conversations with my father, but I wasn't applying the recordings and realizations. It's like journaling and writing down things we say we want to do but never doing them. I realized I wasn't doing anything because every time I smoked, I was saying the same things.

I wasn't getting down to the nitty-gritty of executing things. Smoking allowed me to slow down, to calm down and think about what I need to do. I needed to start doing the work.

Giving was receiving. I was able to slow down. I decided that if I was going to help the world, I needed to help my father first.

That helped me think bigger and see things differently. It helped me become more of a man, sow my royal oats, and become good at a lot of stuff. I became a nutritional therapist and personal trainer. That's where I got my first client. I had people skills. I had started running six miles daily. I had never run a mile in my life.

I got physically fit and got my mind on track. I was able to think for the first time in my life because when you go to college and school, you never really get the chance to think freely. In school, you just keep going, and then you do extracurricular activities, and you have to live life as well.

The nobles had lots of time back in the day, and that was when religion and different systems came into place because they were the ones with time to create while the majority was working. They were able to think and create. Some took the time to learn how to keep hold of control and authority. The one thing that did progress favorably is civilization. I am happy people face the consequences when they are doing unjust things.

When I left my father and left the women, I fell into the depression that had started to overcome me. That's where we were headed right before covering depression. After those negative thoughts started to penetrate the surface, I started my self-development journey.

SELF-DEVELOPMENT PURSUIT

I needed to shake the cobwebs off this victim mindset or hurt mentality so I could really make a shift.

It was a shift from having a paved path, this solid dream, to going out and taking risks to create a whole different life, a whole new ending. What is risk, though? We live one life. I'd rather take a risk chasing my dreams than to live a mediocre life and live within the norms of society. We are here once, and I want to leave an impact on this world.

My father always says life is a gamble. It's true. Everything you do is a gamble. I slowly started shaking off the cobwebs, waking up, and creating a life for myself. I was focused, or at least getting there more and more. I was trying to figure out how I could work toward this world peace project. How was I going to get out of this awkwardness, this fear and the shyness, through doing real estate?

An extraordinary change was happening in my life. All these opportunities were popping up for self-development. All of my days off, my vacation days, and my sick days, I used for self-development. I used them up within the first four months of work, and then I quit work. I should have used all my sick days before I quit too.

I started my self-development journey with two courses at once. I started with a personal development's Basic workshop. When I started that, it woke up my brain cells. It reminded me of who I was again. I was the first to stand up and volunteer to share. I was the one writing in front of the whole class. I was not scared to put myself out there and do what I had to do to make it through and learn.

On the first day of the Basic program, I learned so many fundamental and important things. There are a few games. They have one called the Red and Black game, which was one of the first activities we did.

In the Red and Black game, I learned so much from reflecting. Something so simple. They split us into two groups, and we had to figure out how we were going to win. I was telling them what the answer was. The thing is, sometimes I instinctively just know the answers, like with organic chemistry. I usually know the answer, but I don't always know why. God, or the universe, gives me these instincts or gives me the answer, but I don't know why it is the answer and how I arrived at it.

I was trying to lead and tell them why and figure it out together. There were so many of us, and we had just met. Everybody was being disruptive and speaking over one another. I shut up. I let it go. I stepped back. I realized I was backing out, not backing out of leadership, but because I wasn't able to lead, I wasn't supporting either. I started supporting once I observed this. I said little things here and there, and things started coming together without me even having to do much. My voice was heard, even though they didn't look at me when I said my part. I was like, "Okay, let me just sit back." Wow!

During a few other games we went through that weekend, I learned about integrity and showing up and doing what you say you are going to do. When you have the intention, the mechanism will follow.

The Red and Black game was a real eye-opener. During another game, I realized that I trust people a lot. I always give them the benefit of the doubt. I was ready to be vulnerable again in my life, but I had to work to get there.

I was showing as much love as I could, and the momentum started. It started inside of me. I started going on this positive track. Then a week or two later, this real estate program popped up. It was a class to enhance our performance, and this was the first time it was being offered in Brooklyn for this firm, and I wanted to do it. They gave us the option to pay $800 out of pocket, and they would reimburse us for every sale. I got back $400, but I didn't have another sale after that. That was a while down the path.

I had that sale before I even started the class. It didn't close until later. I was going through the Real Estate workshop series, and in my fourth or fifth week, I took the personal development's Advanced course. When I took Advanced, my life started shifting again. I realized how I was showing up in the world. I didn't even realize that I was showing up in a cool and casual way, not taking full advantage of life. In Advanced, I was challenged to be a mime and to run for hall room monitor president.

This showed me that sometimes I go for the challenge of being president for no payment. That's what Toastmasters showed me. I was working toward the Distinguished Toastmasters (DTM) level, but what is a DTM? Don't get me wrong, I still wanted it. I only needed to mentor one club. I had already done all the work. I had already reached Advanced Communicator Gold (ACG) and had won both the high speaking achievement and the highest leadership achievement.

I was right there, so close. I got excited, and I felt like I was doing something important. We are social creatures, so I was happy to be accepted and growing. The lesson was that sometimes I come off too casual and cool about life. That is what the program pointed out to me. I was playing small. If you play cool and casual, you are not seizing the opportunities of life. You will go through life, and opportunities will pass you by. I saw that happen within my life. I allowed Toastmasters to distract me from creating wealth as a real estate agent instead of making it an asset. As I say this, I feel I'm still being casual sometimes, and I have to get even more on point.

I feel this inside of me right now. The personal development workshop helped me to create a contract for myself to avoid being cool and casual.

My contract is that I'm a humble, urgent, giving leader. I am still working to live by that. I work to be humble by listening and giving praise to God and those in my life. I work to be urgent by staying on top of my work and seizing opportunities. I work to be giving, not with money alone, but with giving people my time and attention, which I can never get back.

This doesn't mean to be giving in a material sense because I have always been a giver in that way. One thing I would say that I wasn't giving people was my time. I wouldn't give my focus, my presence to people. I would just give them things, but I wouldn't give them myself. I learned I had to give myself more as a person, listen to people, and focus on them like I used to when I was going out with girls. They would feel like they were the only one in the room. That's why people love me because I focus on them. I give them what they need. How do you spell *love*? T-I-M-E and devoted attention.

In that experience, I learned a whole bunch of amazing things.

The last one I will share is one of the most impactful lessons to me. I do not want to ruin the course's content. One challenge during the course put us in a hypothetical life-or-death situation that showed us how we save others versus how we save, or choose, ourselves. I chose (and saved) myself, and thank God I did because no one else chose me. These two girls complained about only getting chosen four times. They complained and as everyone gave them perspective, I felt the urgency to offer mine.

I told them, "No one gave me a stick. I choose that I matter and that my life is important, no matter what anyone thinks. I choose to be someone and help others. I believe in myself and know I am here for a purpose."

I ended up writing my two weeks' notice of leaving my EMS job. Well, more like two-month notice. I told them that I loved the company but that I would like to go per diem. But either way, I was leaving. They let me go completely.

They were supposed to give me per diem, but it didn't matter. Whatever happened, happened.

The Advanced course came around my last week of work.

I was in real estate as well. I was sort of doing the work, but I wasn't living in my highest integrity. I was saying that I was making my one hundred required calls per week, but it wasn't always one hundred. I would fill in the paper as if I did, and I was the captain. I wasn't following through. I felt like I could do it. So I wrote things down, but I wasn't actually tracking. Am I tracking right now in my life? I should get more on point and track stronger.

Sometimes we build things in our mind and do not do the work in reality. "What is easy to do, is just as easy not to do" (Jeff Olson)

We think we are—if we tracked, we would be certain we are—and that is why we do not have results. I should focus on what I'm doing and where I'm going to prove to myself that I am doing what it takes to make this thing happen. That is another thing I'm realizing right now. I was tracking my goals, but was I doing enough? If I was really doing a hundred calls per week, I'm sure I would have had the results to reflect that.

The real estate and personal development were going on simultaneously. This lady, Clarissa, in the personal development woke me up; she was hitting at the inner me. One good saying she shared was, "Always leave a place better than you found it."

To me, that is my life as well. I want to leave my friends, family, and the world better off than when I found them.

Journaling about my experiences helped me so much. It's such a valuable tool, just journaling, remembering the real things, the lessons you learn, so you can reflect on them later. It helps you become a better person. Once you write something down, it gets more ingrained in your mind. Someone said, "The strongest memory is not as strong as the weakest ink."

We cannot always remember what we think but having it written down helps. When you write something down, it changes; you keep it forever. When that thought pops up in your mind, it is not always going to stay there.

At this time, I was an area director, and I was vice president for my club at Toastmasters. Wow, this is exactly what Advanced was talking about. My Advanced was April 13. My friend's mom had passed away the same day, years before. I was working on being a hallway monitor, metaphorically. And being a mime in my own life. They taught me how to imitate other people without speaking. What is a mime? Does that symbolize that I was performing and not vocalizing what I feel? What does it mean in my life right now? Maybe it means to stop watching others and imitating them, to speak for what I believe is right. To be myself and work on the dreams I have? Express my desires? Who knows?

I wasn't fulfilling my goals. I was working for the organization, volunteering, but I wasn't doing what I needed to do for my own life. I was giving my life away. I learned a lot of lessons, which blessed me a lot. I was teaching a meditation class as well. My monk, Geneva, called me to come out to work with her at the same time I was going through my troubles.

That December or January, I started teaching meditation sessions in the city. Working with Geneva, I held a meditation session every other Tuesday. It was very effective. She wanted me to do sessions every Tuesday. I usually had eight to ten guests in a room that could fit twenty people. I started connecting with people and teaching them lessons, especially when I led the class. I was using the lessons I wrote about in my book: the gratitude lessons, the things I was learning about chanting, meditative benefits and how to change your mindset and push yourself to a place of abundance.

Wow, I never realized that until right now that I was working to be a hallway monitor president instead of doing my own things that I needed to do in my own life.

I wanted to give up weed that weekend. I didn't feel like smoking at all. My vibration was so high after I got cradled by my team and listened to "Time of My Life." I felt on fire.

The highs.

BACK DOWN, THE INTERMISSION, THE LOWS

I went to Denver, Colorado, the week after the Advanced weekend. Biggs had moved out there. I hadn't seen Reggie in a year since I went to Miami the year before to let Reggie know he had support mentally, emotionally, and physically; we were there for him. So I went to go see both of them. Reggie was meeting me there, and we were staying at the Hyatt. I rented a car. I went and met Biggs. We smoked a little bit. I got super high from this thing called a dab.

It was my first time trying it. I smoked way too much on that trip. I didn't get to experience as much of the city as I wanted. I still had a good time and connected with my friends. We went to a gun-shooting range and a Budweiser brewery.

We ate food and enjoyed our time. We went to a strip club. It was all such a blur because I smoked so much. It was even hard to get out of bed.

When I came back from Advance, I was on a high, and smoking weed, which was supposed to get you high, put me on a low. I went on this lower vibration for a bit. After that trip, I would get up and try to do my calls again. I had already signed up for the next personal development course, their Art of Leadership program, which was starting in June. May was coming up soon.

EQUANIMITY

After Denver, I had a ten-day meditation retreat set up for myself. That was going to be a phenomenal experience. It was going to be over my birthday, ending on the thirteenth or fourteenth. I had gotten a car in December, so I was driving down to Delaware with two other people and excited to go. On the retreat, I saw how much I—and every guy that I roomed with the first four days—had to get over women. They, too, thought about women a lot. I was picturing women I had slept with over the previous two or three years and all the pornography I could imagine. I was having wild fantasies. I felt sad about my first breakup for the entire second day. My first relationship was so sad, and it hurt.

One of the guys had a shirt that said, "Be more legendary," and I was seeing it as I meditated. It allowed my mindset to grow even more because I was trying to figure how to do this world peace project.

Then the thoughts elevated to creating a movie and how I could do all the other necessary things behind it, just from seeing "Be more legendary" while meditating, it was a good mantra. I tried to meditate during all the scheduled sessions. Out of the nine and a half hours of meditation, I probably missed an hour to two a day at most. I tried to do as much as I could.

I straightened my back for a long time. I would have these shaking experiences, almost shivering, after my meditations. When I would go lay down and relax, my whole body would shake and vibrate. I am not sure if it was a Kundalini experience or what. The guys at the retreat said I was very physically active and that I had to be careful and make sure I was taking care of my body.

That ten-day experience was strengthening. I was a vegetarian for ten days. Two days before my birthday, we had birthday cake, a chocolate one. On the ninth day, the day after my birthday, the men and women all connected for the first time, and we were able to talk and interact. At that moment, I realized how much talking overwhelmed us.

When I came back home, since my birthday had just passed, my mom made burgers because they were my favorite.

I didn't want to eat meat again, especially red meat. But since my mom made it for my birthday, I ate it. At that time, I only ate meat twice a week.

I started watching a TV show series about a school teacher who became a drug lord. I remember a girl from college had mentioned it. She said it was so good. A lot of people said it reminded them of me because I was a biochemist. They said I should watch it and told me how it was so phenomenal. I binge-watched the whole series in four or five days. I finally understood what binge-watching was. It was a cool experience. I stayed in my room and just came out to eat. I would stay up practically all day and all night. I would sleep maybe four or five hours and go back to watching it. I wanted to do other things, but I wanted to finish this show so bad. So I binged through it.

I never did that again.

Leadership was coming up soon. I had closed my deal. I allocated ten grand when I left my job.

I needed a spark to go kill this real estate endeavor. It was a totally different thing. It was about asking for what you want, going out there, and doing the work. Sometimes you didn't even feel you deserve what you're asking for, and you feel like you're harassing people. I didn't want to harass people or bother them. I didn't realize I was being a gift. Any service you provide is a gift. Don't worry about what other people think. People will always judge you.

I was coming from a job mindset mentally, where people judge you for your ideas and pursuits outside of that job function.

Real estate showed me what freedom and time could look like.

I had never felt as free in my life. My mom did not bother me at all. I would still go by my father's place. I started biking back to see him that summer. I would bike there and back. I still wanted to be around him to try to motivate him to do more positive things. I started teaching yoga in the park and doing my meditation sessions in Midtown. The meditation sessions kept me grounded, humble and abundant because I had to give from a place of love and gratitude without receiving any compensation.

The leadership program started. The ninety days of leadership was a fun time. I did many things. Each person on our team set goals in categories that pushed us to transform all areas of our lives, from friends and family, spirituality, and community service to finances, education, physical activity, and hobbies.

I had a whole bunch of goals written out, feeding off ideas of the other forty-eight people. I was going toward my dreams and realized I wanted to fix my relationship with my mom. When I got in trouble in my younger years, that affected my whole family and all my friends. During the program, I called everybody—all of my friends and my family—and I apologized to them because when one person messes up, it messes up everybody else, especially the people that are associated with you. They are judged because you are part of their lives and associations. They were still my best friends and loved ones. I felt bad that I let people down.

On the first day of the ninety days, I learned so much. I learned why I was in this state of not wanting to ask for things. I had a mental blockage. Since I was a young kid, my mom struggled. All of my mom's money went to providing a life for us. I saw over twenty mice in our apartment; we lived above a restaurant. When we were growing up, we had just enough food and resources. That's where I got this overeating habit because I felt we did not have enough for everyone. I had a scarcity mindset, but God (the universe) always provides us with enough.

That led to emotional eating and different issues. From a young age of four or five, I realized that I didn't want to ask people for too much. Everyone already had their own challenges, and I did not want to be more of a burden. I tried to give more than I asked for. I didn't ask for clothes or gifts. I got hand-me-downs from my cousin and my brother. I was happy and grateful the whole time, and my mom got me whatever other necessities I needed. I did not see or acknowledge my lack. It is an observation of how my thoughts affected my growth. There was a big blockage. I cared about everybody else. I guess I learned it from my mom. She gave us her all.

A lady on my team asked me, "What about you? Don't you deserve to be happy and have fun?"

She said, "It's time you find a girlfriend, maybe."

I said, "Okay."

I had all these goals set up. I had to run eighteen miles. I had to write a book, make over $100,000 in real estate, and so on.

I could have made that hundred thousand in real estate, but I didn't believe in myself enough. I could have made that hundred thousand in three months, but I wasn't getting up and seizing life. I was still being casual and cool. I feel like I'm still doing that right now in my life. I needed to get focused, get a new perspective, reflect, and make things happen. It was time to stop playing around and believe in myself. My team pushed me to think about how to make money, strategize, and go make it happen.

I would give myself motivational speeches: "You're one of the most powerful dudes you know, Jay, come on. You can do anything. Wake up. Do this. Stop sleeping on yourself. You don't need another job. Go make this money. You have your other business, to make profits. You have free flight benefits. Go to Atlanta and go do this speaking event. Stop playing around, Jay."

That was something I told myself often. "Stop being cool and casual, Jay."

Be humble, urgent, and giving. Give of yourself. Take care of yourself. Meditate, listen to inspiring audios, and grow yourself. Read, exercise, and eat right. I don't think that is being selfish. Even if you do have to be selfish, don't stay there.

I love that line between being selfish, then self-full, and then selfless. You have to take care of yourself and become content; the overflow will then serve others.

Selfish. Think about the word: *sell fish*. Teach a man how to fish. Don't just give them a fish. So go get selfish. Go get the fish for yourself. Fill yourself up so you can help other people. If we don't take care of ourselves, how many people can we help?

Health is taking care of yourself. I tell parents all the time that you have to lead by example. Meditative practices bring you to peace, compassion, understanding, love, and joy. If we want world peace, that's the first place it starts, in our heart and mind.

We have to come to peace within ourselves.

This is vital. I tell the teachers, the parents, and staff this.

Then eating and exercising affect your body. Taking care of your body gives you a positive, high vibration. You release endorphins, which are natural pain relievers, reducing stress and pains. When you take care of your health, you become more confident. With confidence, you tend to treat others better. The way you carry yourself is going to affect your mindset. It is going to bring out a different energy. I would rather my mom be around when I get older than overwork herself and not be here to enjoy the good times. I have to stay focused on this as well for myself.

When your body and mind are aligned, you connect more with your intuition and can create the results you want in life.

On this journey, I did start doing a lot of this. I was meditating daily, working out. I started writing a little bit to teach the meditation classes, which helped to produce the first book.

I had gone down two blocks with flyers for real estate, and one guy threatened to kill me. He was funny. I don't know if that scared me, but it made me feel awkward, like I was bothering people because of what had happened with this guy.

I knocked on his door, so he buzzed me in. His name was Rob. I know him now. He buzzed me in, and I didn't see him. He was up the stairs. He was like, "What do you want?" He thought I was somebody else.

I said, "I'm from up your block. I'm your neighbor. I just started doing real estate."

He said, "Get out of here before I shoot you."

When I saw him the next time, I said, "Hey, you know, I was the guy that rang your bell."

He said, "Next time you ring my bell that early in the morning, you better be bringing $2 million in a briefcase. It was 8:00 a.m."

I thought, *Why wouldn't I just buy his house, both houses, and create a condo if I was spending that sort of money?*

My mom and I went up to Canada to reconnect and strengthen our bond. I met all the goals I had with my family. I went on a trip with my mom, had a good time, and met her family, including Aunty Naf, my mom's aunt. We drove around and took her to a popular aquarium. Her family took us out to eat. I paid because they allowed us to stay for free at their home. We had a good time.

When we were driving back, my mom passed our exit. I was sleeping because I thought I was going to drive the next eight hours back. We started arguing for some reason. I can't remember why we started fighting. I noticed the sun was shining down through the clouds, and it felt like God was shining his light on me.

I said to myself, "Wow, the world is shining on us. Wake up."

I started driving when we stopped to fill up on gas. We drove all the way to Niagara Falls, where we wanted to go on a boat together. We went on a boat; it was one of the last two boats of the night.

There were fireworks set up, which was special. They told us they usually didn't do that. As I sat on the boat looking up at the fireworks with my mom, there were a whole bunch of girls around me.

I looked at her and realized this was a perfect moment. On the ninety-day leadership journey, we were looking for perfect moments. And we just fell in love. I said, "Love you."

She said, "Love you."

I was casual about how I expressed my love.

"Love you," not even "I love you." We went to Hard Rock Cafe afterward. My mom drove back most of the way. I was tired. I don't know how my mom drove those eight hours back practically by herself. I probably drove an hour on my own. She drove most of the time; she has a strong mentality.

The ninety-day journey was coming down to the wire. About six weeks before the end, I started writing about myself, trying to figure out what I could write for the book. I was working on doing a vision board party as well. I was in a mastermind group. I was going to write a story about my life, which I'm doing now in this book. But for the first book, I asked myself, "Why am I writing about my life?" Yeah, sure. It's a cool story. It may touch a few people and help, but I felt I didn't have enough success in life or wisdom. In the end, the book was called *Abundance, a Journey from Anxiety and Depression.*

I was still deciding on what to write. One day, I smoked a little bit before a meeting with TJ, a fellow toastmaster and mastermind associate, but he didn't know. We went to a nice place on Fourteenth Street to discuss how we could create the vision board party. As soon as I left him, I guess my creative juices were flowing because the juices flowed right into what I would write out in the seven chapters of the book. I did the outline for the book on audio recording while driving.

I had the outline, but I didn't start writing it yet. I was running, training myself for the eighteen-mile run. I was up to about twelve miles. I was listening to a lot of motivation from Wayne Dyer, Les Brown, Billy Alsbrook, and Tony Robbins, trying to get my mind-set right and stay pumped up. I didn't do too much more in sales. I wanted to; I would do cold calls. I would do them for about an hour sometimes. Then I wouldn't do it for a while. I was very inconsistent. I was consistent with my workouts, though.

I was also adding people on Facebook for real estate, so I could start doing real estate posts. I had never done one real estate Facebook post, to be honest. As I was adding people, this one girl I added liked one of my videos.

This is around the time of one of our leadership events. She liked one of my motivational videos that I was leaving for my team. From there, I looked at her profile, and she looked cute. I said, "Hey, how you doing? What are your visions? And what are your passions?" in one message.

The next day, she answered it. Guess she had to give it time. We chatted back and forth for a few messages, telling each other what we did. I said, "Hey, you want to chat for a few minutes via telephone?"

She said okay, and we got on the phone, and we started talking. After a while, I said, "Hey, you want to go for lunch?"

She said, "Oh, I'm vegan."

I said, "All right. I was vegetarian for six months before and only ate meat two times a week." She thought I said it just to get with her.

I said, "You want to go for coffee or tea?" She said she drank tea. I asked, "Okay, so where can we meet up?"

She told me about a Starbucks where we could meet. We set up our meeting. Before we hung up the phone, she asked, "Why did you hit me up?"

I answered, "'You are ambitious…and cute." I knew I was not supposed to say that. I knew the field.

She said, "Oh, well, we could network."

I know once she saw me, she was going like me. I didn't care.

"Alright, let's network."

We met up the next day, and I was about five minutes late.

I didn't think traffic was going to be that bad. I walked in and saw her waiting for me, looking at the door. Thinking about it, she was eager.

She walked up to me and said, "You are late. You would have missed the flight."

I said, "You would have held the plane for me." I gave her a kiss on the cheek, and we ordered drinks. I remember the price was $5.12, my birthday. I paid for it. We started chatting. She let me talk. She was a very good listener. I told her my story. We sat on a couch upstairs.

She was a cool girl. I realized how beautiful her eyes were.

I could look into her eyes for the rest of my life. It reminded me of being by the fire in Costa Rica and remembering the feeling of growing old with somebody, seeing their inner beauty. That is how I felt. Veni's eyes were mesmerizing, and I could see right into her. She said that when I looked into her eyes, it was like I was looking into her soul. I'm pretty good at doing that. We talked for about two hours. I knew where it would have gone if we stayed together too much longer. It was not about anatomy. Our chemistry was growing in seconds. She had to go drop her father to the dentist for an appointment that got canceled by the time she got home, apparently.

I walked her out and to her car. My car was by a meter. I had only put two hours on. I already knew how to close the deal. I didn't want to do that with her. I wanted to give her a hug and tell her goodbye, but when I gave her that hug, she stepped in so our bodies were pressing against one other. I had not been with a girl in a long time, nine months to be exact, and my heart started beating faster, and all my blood was flowing. I had recently gone skydiving.

When I went skydiving with my friend Jon, I realized I was going to go after everything I wanted in life. He said he would jump first, but when we went on the plane, I had to jump first. It was only a two-seater with the two guys on our backs.

I know it's a tangent, but that moment reminded me of when we were starting to accelerate before taking off into the air, the guy was trying to slam the door shut, and the door was not shutting. I was like, "Oh my God. Do you want help?" Boom. He hit it once. Boom. He hit it two, three, four times and the door still wouldn't close. I said, "Yo, you want my help. Let me help you." My hands were freer.

He said, "No, no, no, I got it." He finally shut it.

We went up ten thousand or however many feet high up they take you.

He said, "Are you guys ready?"

No. Yeah. Whatever. He popped open the door. I was right near the opening. I had to stand up on the ledge first. I was standing up in the middle of the sky, looking over the clouds, and couldn't see anything visibly on the ground. He said, "You ready? One, two—" And we flew out and into the sky.

I looked at Jon in midair, with a face that said, "What did you get me into, bro?"

As we were falling, I didn't even feel the need to scream, but I started screaming anyway, to let out all that energy. Once I landed, I said, "Jay, go after everything you want in life."

Go after whatever you want. Believe in your dreams and yourself and go after what you want in life.

I jumped out of a plane. I did EMS for four years, which was a never-ending high adrenaline rush. I remember opening up doors of apartments and seeing people covered in blood.

I remember picking up crazy heavy patients who had gone into cardiac arrest, saving some lives. And the times we had to do chest compressions while the families looked at us, crying. All those high-intensity things.

And hugging this girl made my heart beat faster than any of those things. I walked back to my car after the hug, nice and smooth, because if I hugged her any longer, who knows where it would have gone.

I felt this urge. I was nauseated because of all the adrenaline. I guess in society we call it butterflies.

I drove as fast as I could, right to my Toastmasters meeting, just wanting to get away. That night, I went for a crazy amazing six-mile run. Afterward, I called her and we talked.

I invited her to my friend Cassandra's BBQ the next day. That night was the last time I had chicken in my life. I ate a piece of fried chicken after my run.

She made it to the BBQ. My mom said, "Oh, you know she's not going to want to do certain things for so and so reasons." I forget what she said, but whatever line my mom said, I told the girl and it made her want me even more. After the BBQ, we went into the car, and we started making out. She was all on top of me. I knew she wanted it. This was the time and the era. I took her back to the apartment and closed the curtains. I had plans of going to the personal development group that night. I had a dear friend I introduced to the program to support.

I went to go enjoy my friend's experience, and he was not even there. He canceled three times in a row. I was out with the girl late that night, and I said, "Hey, I got to leave."

We had fun, at least I didn't do it on the first date. Two days later, I went to her house. She let me in. She had cooked some stir fry for me. I never asked a girl, from the genuineness of my heart, to be my girlfriend. They usually ask me. I asked her, and she said yes.

From there, I wanted to meet her father because he was in the room, but she didn't want me to meet him. She said he was a grump. That night, I ended up dropping her off to pick up her mom because her car would give her trouble sometimes. She had a red drop-top

Mustang. I met her mom. I went to give her a kiss on the cheek. She tried to dodge it, and I hugged her at the same time. She didn't dodge that too much.

That same week, I watched my niece. I went to the gym every day. I wrote the first book in about twelve hours, even while this girl and I started fighting for no reason.

I ran the eighteen miles I intended to run. All these things were happening at once. She put the spark back in my life. I didn't want to waste her time. I didn't want to waste my time.

The eighteen miles really helped me get over a lot of jealousy issues from my past relationship. We told each other our whole life stories. We were really bumping heads in the beginning. I felt it was going to be a temporary, transitional relationship. We were using each other to get to the next side.

That's when we met our mentor, Josiah, and a series of events started happening from there.

I'm going to talk about that and the next few turns that happened in our life.

THE SECOND CHANCE

Veni is very ambitious, hardworking, and positive. That was one of the main things I liked about her, her positivity, and her pretty brown eyes.

She worked super hard, every single day. Either she was going to the gym and leaving her house at 3:30 a.m. to open the gym before five, or she was working a flight. She didn't show any fatigue, but I could feel it was draining her. I didn't really want her to do the job too much, especially when we started the business. She was a flight attendant. She worked seventy to eighty hours a month. She was studying to be a health coach, which was taking up some of her time. She was also working at the gym. She was doing three things and now us. It was a lot.

As soon as we met, she had been having car troubles with her Mustang, which she really wanted to keep. She had wanted it for a long time, but she was very vague about what she desired. Her request wasn't specific. She got a drop-top red Mustang, but it was not in the best condition. Something was wrong with her fuel pump or fuel injector. After the first week of us going out, I was giving her my car keys to drive to work. I had never let anyone drive my car, only my big sister when she moved it for me one time.

We started hanging out more. My brother was leaving the following week to head to a Nickelodeon cruise ship. This was the second or third trip he wanted me to watch his dog for the week, which was also the week of Veni's birthday.

I asked her what she wanted for her birthday. She had mentioned a few things. She said that she had never been to a Broadway play. I said, "Do you want to go to one? Which one would you like to go to?"

While we were on the phone, I bought the tickets.

In disbelief, she screamed, "No!" We had only been going out for one week at that point. I wasn't sure if we would make it to that time. We were getting rocky, especially after I was trying to edit my book and do other things. Resistance was happening, a term from *The War of Art*.

The War of Art really explains this topic of resistance, especially when you are an artist or a writer. I saw this happening each night we bickered about something, when I was writing my first book. I would have one of my great nightly workout sessions with a friend. I would want to go write but end up talking to her until all my energy was drained. I gave the book the bare minimum attention. We would fight for an hour or two. Not fight but discuss little things. It wasn't good for the relationship. It wasn't good for her. It was her mindset. She would complain about her jobs, and I can't even remember what else, to be honest. It was nothing big, but it was draining. It was probably me. I was probably trying to create this perfect person.

That week is when she met Josiah, our mentor.

The whole week, she was at my brother's house with me, and when we were together, we got along. We went out that whole week. Even the day of her birthday, we didn't really have time, but we went somewhere. Then I dropped her off at her house. I had to shoot over to my brother's house and walk the dog. I set up the whole house. I had one hour, maybe an hour and twenty minutes. The drive alone is twenty minutes each way.

I stopped and got rose petals and threw them on the bed. I got candles, took off the stickers, which took some time. I had about six to eight candles and put them all over. I put two to four in the bathroom and put rose petals in the bedroom, trickling them down to the hallway. I kept the dog out of the bedroom. I set everything up. I had to shower, get ready, and leave to pick her up. I had picked up flowers when I bought the rose petals. I was five or ten minutes late to pick her up to go to the show. I was determined to make it on time. I'm a guy that leaves early for everything. When I arrived to pick her up,

I saw her standing by the window waiting for me. She was like an excited little schoolgirl when her crush comes to visit.

She was looking for a love like mine. She was excited. We were like teenagers. I came and gave her the flowers. We took some pictures. It felt like prom. We went to the city early and ate at the Brooklyn diner. We got a vegan burger and had a good time. Then we went to the play.

We had really good seats. We saw a couple leave the side section on the balcony, and I said, "Let's go sit there."

We went and sat there, but it wasn't as good as our seats. But it was okay; we were already seated. We enjoyed it from there. It was more about taking in the moment and the experience of being together. Our first Broadway play.

As we were driving home later that night, we saw an accident on the road.

"Babe, I'm sorry. I'm going to have to stop." This big truck was flipped over on its side. I had just stopped being an EMT like four or five months prior. It was in my nature. I did not have my utility knife to break the glass. I jumped out, looked into the cab of the truck, and saw that all three people were fine. I didn't really want to interfere with the scene. Before I got out of the car, I said, "Hey, babe, call 911 and tell them exactly where we are."

She told them where we were and which exits we were between. Other people had called the cops already, but I wanted to make sure they got the call and the right address. I saw that everybody was good. No one was unconscious; everybody was functioning. I let it rock, and I kept moving. Once the cops and EMT got on scene, I went home. I asked her to go on the balcony for a second. I lit the candles in the room. I started the water in the bathroom and put some rose petals in the tub and lit more candles. I told her, "Hey, let's go take a bath."

She saw the rose petals and started getting emotional. I had gotten a non-alcoholic beverage and two wine cups. We had it while relaxing in the tub, laying back. I had a rag to wash our bodies, and she laid back on my body; it was an intimate night.

Next week, she met Josiah on Tuesday when I had a meditation session, so I couldn't go. They met at a luxurious gym where Veni used to work. Professional basketball players went there because they have a full-size basketball court. Even popular pop artists went there. The gym was very high-end. Even I went there.

This guy came in while she was there one day. She didn't have a particular position yet because nobody was on staff to assign her. Josiah walked in and said, "Oh, I came to look at the apartments."

She said, "Well, this is the gym. I can give you a tour of the gym." And she gave him a tour of the gym.

She asked, "What do you do?"

He said, "I help people retire in their twenties and thirties. I help them with financial independence."

She said, "Okay, I'm becoming a health coach. Can you teach me how to budget my money?"

He said, "All right."

He took her and Alyssa's numbers, but Alyssa, Veni's coworker, didn't answer when he called. So he ended up calling Veni about her friend Alyssa. Veni and Josiah ended up meeting about the budget session on that Tuesday when I had the meditation session.

I couldn't attend because I'm very loyal to what I do. When they sat down, he helped her, and then he talked about the people he knew that had retired at twenty-eight. She talked about me, and he was like, "Well, I want to get to know him."

She said, "I want to get to know those other people." I met up with her again on a Saturday. It was the same day I first met her brother, who they say is the real father of the family. I met the brother because we were dealing with her Mustang, which was giving her trouble again. One day that week, when I was at my brother's house, she called me while she was driving to work with her mom and said, "My car broke down."

I said, "Babe, what do you want me to do? Call Triple A. Why did you call me? I'm going to come there with my car and pull your car."

I asked her if she wanted me to come. She said no. I said, "Veni, do you want me to come?" She said okay.

So I drove over there for no reason. Thank God I found parking for free. Everything ended up working out. I waited for her to get off of work, which was within an hour because she had to go fix her car.

The next day, we went out to fix the car and take it to another shop, after she had already spent over $200 at one place, wasting her money.

That day, I went with her brother to the car dealership. I got to meet her sister-in-law as well. That was a funny experience. We went to a few shops. One place that said they could sell the car for us. They said that if they made more profit, they would give it to us. I was dressed down. I had on a polo, short pants, and shades, chilling out.

We took it to a few other shops. At the last one, the mechanic was making jokes. He said, "Hey, you want to take him out back? We could take him out back." He was talking to the brother.

Her brother looked at me. I said, "I'm good. I will take you both."

That was it for the tension. Things became more solid right there because I wasn't scared. Later that day, we met up with Josiah. When I met him, I was already looking at this guy, thinking in my head, *You went out for coffee with my girl*, but he was super respectful.

We chatted and got to know each other. One thing I didn't like about the whole situation with them meeting up was that she canceled my meditation session to meet him. It is all good, though.

As we talked, he gave us a book to read. Next, he showed us an opportunity.

I realized by the way he presented it to us that it was something I could do. Everything was up-front, and people got the right education to understand how the opportunity works.

It was a business opportunity that would allow me to not have to go to school and not go through the politics of society, where I could actually cultivate my dreams and do the things I wanted to do.

My purpose is to join the world and work to end suffering, making sure everyone has food, water, shelter, and clothing, expanding it on to holistic healthcare and education. I want to inspire the young and those who have given up on themselves. I realized through time and continuously hitting goals that I really want to enjoy my journey and that charity starts at home.

I will make sure my family is comfortable and that we have a good life, that we can enjoy life's luxuries, and that everyone is content. Josiah showed me this opportunity that helped me realize I could create that. We kept going through a process together and getting to know each other more. He told us about talking about our visions and our values with each other. He didn't tell us to do it, but he said another successful couple did it, teaching indirectly.

One time Veni said she did not get to go to this cool Thai restaurant when her friends went for their birthdays. She wanted to go, but she wasn't telling me she wanted me to take her there. She didn't think I would remember. I said, "Let's go there for lunch slash dinner."

We went and talked about our visions and values. She told me what she wanted. I told her what I wanted. I told her, "I don't want to be separated from my mother and my family. I know some girls pull guys away from their families. I just want to be a part of their lives. I have seen it happen with some of my friends, and if that happens, I will resent you." I told her I was a workaholic and that if we needed to take a break, we should make sure we take a break.

"If you ever feel like I'm neglecting you or something, tell me to slow down. Lastly, I'm committed to working on this world peace project."

I explained that it was something I was dedicating my life to. If we couldn't make time for that, it wasn't going to work. She agreed to all the things I wanted. She wanted to help her family, travel the world, and stuff like that. I know she would show me a better view of life, a more luxurious view. Women make life more beautiful. We decided to collaborate and build together.

That's the path we went on. We made it through the process and started mentorship. When we sat down with Josiah. He said, "Jay, if you want to do all these things, the first thing you have to do is change yourself. And if you want to grow a big business, you've got to grow yourself."

Okay, sounds good. So we started doing just that.

Once we began mentorship and regularly reading and listening to talks and reading books, our lives started changing dramatically.

What I think really kicked off our life in a major way is that we were bullet journaling. We were tracking our days. We were creating our second business. We were getting up at five in the morning and doing a routine of chanting, meditation, and yoga, and we set up a daily phone call talking to other people also on this spiritual path. We were still holding our meditation sessions.

Those activities kept us grounded.

We were focused spiritually and physically. Physically, it includes both our body and our finances.

We would do that every morning. I would meditate at night for a few minutes and do my gratitude beads as well. It all kept me on track. It got me to the next level, where I was far more focused on my life. With all these positive things in my life, I was able to publish my first book in a month.

My mom showed it off at her school that first month after I published the book. I spoke with the school's parent coordinator, and I created a curriculum to teach. When Veni and I had our first talk in the schools, they hired us on the spot. I went on many speaking engagements. As soon as I got that book published, I contacted all the Toastmasters Clubs and told them I wanted to speak about the book. I made a decent number of sales on that within Toastmasters, even though you are only supposed to sell at certain events. But you could sell outside of the venue to people who were leaving. I was getting a lot of exposure. We went to a health coaching conference out at the Fairmont Hotel in Dallas, Texas. It was a very nice experience.

Meanwhile, Veni and I fought like crazy. It was little things she was doing, but the problem was that I needed attention and was spending a lot of money as well. I suffered a lot from not getting enough attention, probably because I did not get it from my mom and dad.

I do not remember getting much affection, hugs, or compliments growing up. If I did, it was a scarce amount. I could understand that my mom was working hard while raising children. She had to be a single mom and has worked hard my whole life, so far. I guess that is how she showed her love.

Veni and I fought, but we were growing. We were fixing the relationship. Then with Josiah, we were still self-developing, individually. Within the first three months of self-development, we published books, and I had twenty-plus speaking engagements. We had to incorporate our small business, Body, Mind, and Soul, which will become a nonprofit and expand globally down the line.

We were developing a curriculum for that, learning how to execute each focus area, fine-tuning our process, so we could bring our project to the masses. We started in the schools and were getting paid for it. I had to set up our LLC for that. We had a retreat in the Dominican Republic. We scheduled three retreats, and we marketed them on a few websites, but we didn't get any callbacks. We had two potential leads that we could have secured, but we didn't book it out. We should have just paid somebody 10 to 15 percent to handle bookings for us. That's what we will do next time. We will have to make the prices higher to allocate those percentages.

We didn't book any of the three retreats. What else did we do? She was about to start her ninety-day leadership journey. At this time, she was going through a lot of stress. She was working on a vegan cookbook. That started after she had been talking about how she wanted to do a vegan cookbook. I said, "Well, your mom's cooking right now. Why don't you go and get a pen and paper and start now?" When she began with her leadership group, she started writing her book and focusing on it as one of her primary goals. We trained to run sixteen miles.

It was a week before the year ended. I was still determined to have a retreat, even if we had to use our buddy passes and break even. I wanted to throw it.

I called Veni into the bathroom. I said, "Hey, babe, come please." I was showering. I told her, "Babe, I want to throw this retreat within the next week."

She said, "No, I have work."

I said, "Damn, before you even listen, you are shooting down my dreams."

She said, "But I have work."

"You're shooting down my dreams for work?" I said. "Get out of here. I am going to call somebody else." I called this other girl she and I knew from Facebook.

We had talked a few times. I called and explained everything to her. She said, "Okay, I'll help you sell out these retreats."

You could see Veni's wheels spinning. She didn't say anything. That shut her down. We were going to do it. I was going to have her help me. Then Veni got on board, and she got one girl to commit, paying the full price. Then I had three other people commit to paying $600 each since it was three of them in one shot. Then the last guy, I lost a bit of money. I charged him the least because he was a friend. I spent $100 out of my own money.

The week before the end of the year, I declared that we would have this turn out in our favor. We got all the money together the day before our trip. I tried to book three different places because the website said it would take twenty-four hours for hosts to confirm. By the time we landed, all three requests were denied.

After landing, I turned around and told everybody, "Hey, I tried to book a few places at the last minute last night, and they all got canceled as soon as we landed. I tried to book two or three of them, but don't worry. We'll find a place."

Some of them had panic in their faces.

I walked outside. Thank God Yaya, one of the girls traveling with us, spoke Spanish. I said, "Hey, let's ask some of these people if they know of anyone who has any villas?"

One person we asked said they knew of one. They showed us the villa via pictures and told me the price.

They called the owner, who said yes, it was available. When I met with him, I negotiated the price down a few hundred dollars. He gave us the whole house. It was magnificent and beautiful, with a pool in the backyard, a guard on-site, and a coconut tree. They needed half an hour to finish cleaning. It was a five- to ten-minute walk from the beach. It was a beautiful place in between Sosúa and Puerto Plata, Carmen del Playa.

Every day, we ate lunch and dinner somewhere new. I changed up the scenery each day within this one home. I should have been more assertive through the experience to do the work. We made it through most of the curriculum. I sent out the itinerary, but I was a little casual with time and should have kept a stricter schedule. It was still a great event.

I gave them a lot of tools. I feel like I blessed them a lot. Veni, the head of marketing, did a great job recording things and setting up what we needed. Veni had published a vegan cookbook. I was able to become a life coach because the book I published put me in that category.

I wanted to get certified as a life coach because we were going to start speaking in schools, and I didn't want credentials to hold up our progress. I took a course that was supposed to take three to six months. I did in one month. All of this happened in three months. We were marinating and ready to move.

We attempted to introduce two people to our financial independence business. Josiah told us, "Not yet," because we had things left to get in order. We were getting a little frustrated about that. It was taking our mind off the business, but he was very consistent. That is what made me commit to doing the business.

When one of the larger leaders in our organization came, we committed to introducing one new person to our business idea once a day. That's when our business started taking off. We started talking to people every day, and in the next six months, we had six people on our team.

Those people did not stick around because we needed to develop our leadership skills, see the value of mentorship, and learn a lot more. We needed to work out the kinks and iron out the phases of our operation.

Next, I started working with my mom and sister, some of my new best friends, my fraternity friends, and some former strangers. It took those first six people dropping out for me to realize I had growing and learning to do. And that's what really helped me last in the business. I said to myself, "Wow, if I really want to help the world, I've got to be able to love and slow down and learn how to serve people."

I thought I loved people, but I didn't realize that loving people means being patient, like good parents. These are our business kids. It's the same thing. Thank God for our parents.

I had to learn to be patient with myself and with my girl. When I started staying with her, we started bickering every night.

At the beginning of our relationship, the first two times I came into the house, I heard that her father had told her brother, "Oh, this guy's coming into our house and hasn't said hi to me yet."

I tried to say hello to him, but Veni told me not to. One day we came in, and I said, "Go say hi to your dad." She didn't greet him regularly.

She went to say hello, and I shouted from the living room, "That guy is here as well."

Her mother and father's relationship got better as well. I told her that once I came into the house and we started doing this, their relationship was going to get better, and it did. I said that for my own ego, but I know what love does. Love brings love out of other people.

He said he was coming out. He came out, introduced himself, and sat on the couch. He was shaking a lot. I don't know if he was scared of me or what happened. Maybe my spirit shook the bad out of him. Maybe it was his diabetes. We chatted for a bit, and he said, "You're welcome to come over anytime."

I took the invite literally and started sleeping over there very often. That was taking a toll on our relationship because we were always doing business-related things. I was very accountable. I had to tell her to do certain things, but she also had a job. I may not have been understanding. I was working the same number of hours and putting in the same amount of time. She also had to deal with a negative work environment, and I feel that negativity always ends up coming home. She would be in a super positive, upbeat mood before going into work, but that changed by the time she came home every time. We were fighting, and tensions were getting higher. I became verbally abusive again, telling her to shut up and putting her down. We fought a lot and usually for no reason.

Then it started getting physical. Once, she hit me, and I told her, "Oh, you can't hit me. You don't want that kind of physical relationship."

Eventually, when she would hit me, I would hit her back.

Thank God that didn't last too long. Josiah was counseling and helping us figure out what was going wrong and how we could fix it. We set up a time to hang out and counsel with each other and started relationship counseling with Josiah, which I feel was very important. He gave us a lot of tools to help our relationship.

When we were at Veni's house, her ego was very big. It was big in general, especially when she was around her parents. I think her ego was bigger than mine. It makes sense, though. In some Indian cultures, the women run the household. She would say that I didn't want to look bad and that I cared about my reputation. Yet she always had to act a certain way in front of her parents. I was probably doing it with my mom and family as well.

Again, it is easier to see things in others and not see them in yourself. Your eyes look outward, but the only person you can change is yourself. You have to learn to look within and be attuned to yourself as well.

One day, the day after my cousin's wedding, I decided to go back home. I got up and gathered up all my clothes and shoes. I hadn't realized I had that much stuff there. I took everything and put it in my car. My whole backseat was full of stuff. We were fighting and breaking up. She had been texting on a group chat with Josiah and me.

Josiah called me and talked some sense into me. I tried to talk to her again, but she acted very childish. I was upset with her childishness. I went and met with her in the Laundromat. I told her I would pee on her clothes as she was trying to record our conversation. I took the phone and threw it on the floor. Then she called the cops, but I had already dipped. I was thinking, *Damn, this girl is trying to ruin my life.*

That's why I stopped sleeping over there all the time. It took a big dramatic event for us to stop sleeping together. We continued to build and do the things we needed to do for the business.

We ended up fighting again on Christmas. I'm a very timely person. I like to be on time. I knew she could do things that I couldn't do, and I was trying to split up our work. I told her, "Hey, babe. You go do this stuff. I'll do this here."

She went to wash dishes and ended up wasting time. I said, "Babe, I told you not to wash the dishes. Go do that." She was like, "What?" She got loud. Her family probably did not hear. But I saw her ego coming back out again in front of her family. I was like, "Baby, you could just say sorry," and she got even crazier. I told her not to come by my family's place. Her mom was eavesdropping.

I could have let it go or spoken nicer to her. I do not have to confront everything. We sometimes have higher expectations for people around us and do not treat them as we would a stranger.

Her mom got involved in everything. I took the vegan crab cakes I had made and left. I wanted her to come. I stopped and called her. I said, "Please come."

Her mom had that influence on her. The people closest to you can manipulate you very easily. She let her parents get involved in our relationship, but it was my fault either way; we were in their house. How could we not let them get into our relationship? That's why, when I get married, I will work to make sure we live on our own. Yeah, there are a lot of perks living with her parents, like the food and cleaning, but we won't learn how to become strong together and be self-sufficient.

Then Mommy and Nessa went over to Veni's house after they left Sean's house. Imagine my girlfriend, the one with whom I was supposed to be building a future with, her parents and my own mom and sister, talking bad about me. Then everybody started talking badly about Jay. I had to apologize to everybody and said sorry for how I reacted.

I could have reacted better. I was sorry for how I behaved. But at the same time, I thought, *Sorry, I want to punch you in your nose. What the hell is wrong with you people? You're doing the wrong thing, too, but when I reacted badly, I'm the one who's wrong.*

I apologized because Josiah said to apologize. But when I'm right, I'm right. So until Veni admitted it, I wasn't going to speak to her too much. She eventually admitted the truth, and then our relationship started getting better after a few weeks. We went back to building our team, the day after Christmas though I was already prospecting someone new.

I know our life is going to take a dramatic change. We have the momentum. We have the education, and our team is getting stronger. I feel like this year; big life-changing experiences are going to happen.

I am going to be taking a step forward with her, even though she doesn't know it yet. That's where we're headed. I've been wanting to write this book/movie for a while, about a year now, if not more.

One night when we were watching a movie recommended by one of my coaches from the personal development program, Veni said, "How's your book going? Or your movie? Why don't you just write it?"

I got up that night and began to see exactly what to do with the book and the movie, what I would incorporate, and how I would go about it. I saw how I had to take control of my life. It took me about six months to implement those things I talked about that night. It has taken me even longer to set up the next steps in my life to get the results.

I know exactly what I want to do in the book. I want to project how we can help the world and how veganism and vegetarianism or the reduction of meat in general are important. I want to discuss how much meat production is destroying the planet and other major topics like war, violence, religion, sexism, and more. I want to target all these issues and show how we can heal the planet and all its people. I realized how dramatic mass meat production was when I first created my first documentary. I erased it, but I had over one hundred views on YouTube. I had done that as a leadership goal project. The other topics I learned through real life and education and topics I taught in the meditation sessions and schools would all help heal the world.

I see ways to heal the world and make sure the world has enough abundance and that everyone has what they need to create inner peace and world peace. I see how we could go about it and move into a more efficient society, one where we are healing the planet, not destroying it. It involves steps like moving from mass meat consumption to producing more agriculture; creating more supermarkets, schools, and wellness centers; and changing the whole scene of medicine. We can start to heal people in a different way. The money will still be there; society will still prosper. We have to change, and I believe we can over time. If not, those willing to move with change will succeed.

We must offer the companies across various industries the ways to adjust and participate. That's why I'm growing my financial independence business to establish my grounding for my family. I will get the funding and create a nonprofit to help connect and facilitate these initiatives by working with existing organizations and filling in the gaps where needed. We will gain the necessary supporters to produce this movie, draw in a big audience (also known as the world), and raise revenue to support the movement.

I want to make sure I have a solid foundation because if I have to focus on money, I can't focus on advancing these projects to help people and the world, uniting humanity, or helping us love one another.

Sure, people have different lifestyles, and not everybody is going to be on an equal playing field—this will still be a capitalist society—but this can be a place where there is no severe poverty, where people are not chastised out of society and into exile or homelessness. We will learn how to eradicate the sicknesses of drug addiction and how to heal the issues that cause them. The vision includes stopping the segregation of people through religion, healing the planet through good agriculture and wholesome education, viewing all societies and their cultures as contributions to be celebrated.

We must teach people how to cultivate peace within themselves. I will expand this vision dramatically through the book, then the movie, which will both be bestsellers. Once this billion-dollar-revenue-producing movie is out there, I'm donating half the funds to this nonprofit that will work on implementing all these ideas. I will take 10 percent for my hard work, so I can make sure everything is good at home and have the means to focus on improvement and growth for the movement. This is also so I have the time to work out the kinks and make sure everyone else that is involved gets paid well too. I would make sure it is fair.

In the next chapter, I will explain the next steps for changing this planet and identifying the changes we want to bring about in the next two to five years, deciding what we are going to do, and envisioning how beautiful our businesses will be.

I will share and reflect on the things I'm learning through the businesses, what I'm doing with both Body, Mind, and Soul and the financial independence business. I am discovering what it takes to create and perfect it while I'm doing it. On this journey, what is going to change dramatically in my life? I'm excited to explore how things unfold within the next few years as I work toward world peace.

THE DRAMATIC SHIFT

As my life began to shift, I started developing two businesses right away. Veni and I went down a rocky path, but thank God for Josiah for counseling us on our relationship and being an outside voice. Having a coach is like when people watch the quarterback during a football game. They say, "Why didn't he throw it to that person?"

You're not in the game.

It's easy for you to see things when you do not have the pressure on you. That's why I love coaching and having a coach. He could see what was going on in order to help our relationship. I'm thankful that he has developed himself so much and studied healthy relationships so he could help us with ours.

We started building two businesses. Our passion project, Body, Mind, and Soul BMS, started off strong and hard and died down a bit so we could focus on our financial independence business. Body, Mind, and Soul BMS is one of our passions and things we believe should be spread throughout the world. We are definitely going to convert it into a nonprofit and expand it to create a television channel where the curriculum could be shared and implemented in homes. The knowledge can be taught and spread all over.

With Body, Mind, and Soul, its purpose goes back to the basics of living, back to the bare minimum, and that is what we need. Get back to the basics of taking care of yourself, eating right, slowing down, taking a walk or meditating, sitting down in a park, or whatever it is. It's about calming the mind, coming into peace within yourself, loving one another, watching how you speak, focusing on the good in people, and allowing that to come out of them. It's about learning how to coach, how to parent, and how to influence in the right way. Dale Carnegie's *How to Win Friends and Influence People* was the second most sold book in the world because its message is crucial.

It explores how we should treat each other. It's not about trying to influence people for malicious reasons. It is about influencing people in the right direction. I guess that's assuming you have intentions. That's why it's important to develop a relationship with your higher power, whatever it may be, God, the universe, or something else.

I originally started Body, Mind, and Soul to become a personal trainer and a nutritional therapist. I had a client, but I didn't see how to make the business lucrative until I met Veni, and she sparked me back up. When she started doing health coaching, health coaching was popular and people were paying top dollar for it. My book made me a life coach, and I got certified as an Integrative Wellness and Life Coach. My mom initiated this business by introducing us to the Parent Coordinator at the school she works at, but *How to Win Friends and Influence People* showed me how to speak in the right perspective, to connect with people in the right way.

Once we launched that business, we started creating curriculums, and I took suggestions from my big sister, who is a teacher. I didn't create all of it. I made curriculums from the things I had studied and learned. I implemented things I had learned from different areas of my life and put them together in a smooth package, so it would be effective and accessible. Veni helped to create the health coaching curriculum.

I feel like these things are what should be taught in schools. Why do we teach *The Great Gatsby*, teaching about drinking, smoking, having sex, and cheating on people, instead of teaching children to be good, moral people? We should be teaching the youth how to treat one another with love and respect. Body, Mind, and Soul covers all of that. In the Body area, take care of yourself. Exercise but make it fun. Do things you like, something that challenges you. Are you eating right? That doesn't necessarily mean just eating the most nutritious foods, which is the right thing to do, but also consider, how do you eat it? Slow down and get into a relaxed state so you don't have high levels of cortisol as you eat. Cortisol release leads to fat deposits. The lessons include so many impactful things.

For example, chewing, which is a challenge I am overcoming. When I worked as an EMT, I would gobble down my food, just in case we got a call and had to rush out. Breaking the bad habits I had developed was important. We are trained to rush around and not give ourselves enough time. I would rather wake up a little early and meditate than to rush into and through the day and not take that time for myself. We have to put ourselves first. We have to nurture our minds. That is one of the main things we talk about. Body, Mind, and Soul is a reminder to take care of ourselves.

We as humans innately know what we should be doing, and we have heard it many times. Practice is the key, and when you repeat knowledge and are reminded, you are more likely to do what you need to do. We remind people and give them simple tips and techniques from our education to help them make minor changes that will have great impacts in all areas of their lives.

We have to make sure we bring ourselves to peace because if we don't have peace within ourselves, there will never be world peace. This is true for parents, adults, and kids too. As parents and adults, we are influencing these kids. If we don't take care of our energy, even in the workforce, we won't be as successful as we could be. If you want to be successful in anything, you have to take care of your energy.

You can destroy a whole business with a few bad workers who have temper tantrums or a bad leader within the company. It's very important to connect with yourself. Slow down a bit.

People say, "I don't have time to meditate." For me and many other successful people, we get more accomplished when we do meditate because it helps us focus and execute better. I don't have to think as much. I can handle complex situations. It brings me to a place of compassion and understanding so I can give more love to people because love is the way to success.

There are only two forces guiding us: love and fear. You are always leading and being led by one or the other. Learn to lead with love. If you want something to really grow, you have to nourish it.

Nourishment comes from love and care. Fear brings death. Things originate from love or fear. You choose.

With love, I still establish deadlines. I'm not saying that all you have to do is love, and everything will be all right. You have to be focused and follow through. You have to get to that place, but love plays a factor in making that happen. An element of love is belief, faith in yourself. You can set a whole bunch of goals, but if you don't have faith in yourself, if you don't build that strength, they will not come to fruition.

Then came the health coaching, movement, and retreats. We did our first retreat where we implemented this curriculum, helping people find their purpose. We spent time on establishing healthy practices and how to generate a positive mindset with tools such as practicing gratitude, prayer, meditation, journaling, or whatever works to help you stay focused and on target. We explored what is possible when you take care of your mind, keep it positive, clean, and steady.

Now, when you have the body and mind aligned, that is when you allow your soul to be activated, and you achieve your purpose, what your soul truly desires, and your true intuition. That's how I feel, and that's what I see.

You have to take that time to figure out why you're here and what you are trying to do. It doesn't have to be complex; you could want to be a great parent, for example. Just be. It's about being. You have to find out what you want to be. It can be a guy who pumps gas at the gas station. If that is what makes you happy and successful and allows you to provide for your family and do what you need to do, that's what your purpose in life is. That's your purpose. We all play a role on this Earth.

My father once told me, "Jay, someone has to pick up the garbage." We cannot all perform the same functions in society.

There has to be someone that administers the medicine, does surgery, and teaches kids. We all work together. We all play a crucial part.

Humans are all similar, and we make the world go around. As in the body, which is all the same cells, just slightly differentiated, we specialize each in something different but necessary. We are all the same; we just do different things to make the world function.

The world collaborates, even though it has both destruction and unification. We should work more on unifying.

We destroy because of fear. There is fear of not having enough, of needing more. If we were in a love state, we would be abundant and content. As we developed this business more and continued building the curriculum, we learned how to make it better and implement it for different audiences.

I learned about religion when I went to a community center. My mentor, a great guy who understood my point of view, would tell me a lot about Christianity. Then one day in a coffee shop near this church on Forty-Sixth Street, someone told me the only way to be saved was through Jesus and the word. Later, when I went to a mosque to try to speak as a professional on general topics in the community center, a clerk I spoke to was trying to make me become Muslim.

She said, "Oh, there's a reason you're here. You are back to be a part of the mosque."

I thought, *I see how everybody thinks. Is this right?* I figured it was like when you work a job or do anything, you think it is the right thing, the best thing, and you try to get other people into your thing. We do it because we want to give ourselves dignity for what we do.

I believe once you judge another, you go against all religions. We should respect and love all and allow people the same grace, love, and mercy that God and the universe give us. Allow people to believe what they want, not saying people cannot be educated on new topics. If people are judging others, they will be going against their own religions.

I can understand that it is still part of unification. The only thing I oppose about religion is that it segregates us, for example, like color separates us, when in reality, we are all part of the human race. We are all one. Religion has caused the most deaths and wars. Religious institutions own the most real estate and have a large quantity of money. Think about it.

I believe religion is great because it can guide people toward a higher being by believing in something bigger than themselves. It can bring more civilization to society, but when you think that you're better than somebody with differing beliefs, I think that's where it becomes bad. That is when things are affected. We create a superior-versus-inferior dynamic, though no one is better than anyone else. When the Muslim clerk was trying to tell me I had come back for the religion, I realized that everybody thinks what they're doing is the right thing. They say they don't have any opposition toward other people, but it is being shown indirectly. Everybody thinks that their way is the only way. I believe the biggest piece of this all is your mind. You have to make sure that it is positive, that it is pure, and that it is love. I keep learning how to come to peace through the curriculums.

My mentor is Christian and speaks of Jesus a lot. It is his faith. It could have irritated me, but we came to an understanding. We skipped religion and went to spirituality. He says it is important to build a connection and relationship with God. I agree totally.

We do not need church or religion to build a relationship with our higher power or God. To me, that is the truth and the most important. We can all connect with our higher power directly and develop our own relationship. Believing that life and my dreams are bigger than I am and that there is a higher power relieves my anxiety and helps me know I do not have control over everything. I will do the work and let God handle the rest.

That is the reason I spread Body, Mind, and Soul—so we can get back to the basics, stay healthy, eat right, and keep up our practices of being the best person we can be, which includes being mindful of how we treat others and how we treat ourselves.

As we develop and spread Body, Mind, and Soul, I see how we could implement it in wellness centers and how it could heal people. The way we feel and the thoughts we think radiate to so many other people because everything is a vibration. Our thoughts, vibration, and energy frequency spread and emit outward. If you're not at peace in your heart, you're going to destroy families and future generations. Everyone and everything could be destroyed because of your inkling to not take a second to breathe. Breathe and slow down. Allow yourself to come to peace and love. Know you are whole and worthy and let that spread. Your thoughts are a vibration, a transmission that has a frequency. People will feel your energy, whether you try to hide it or not. Clean it up and clear it out. Come to compassion so we can grow in love and abundance.

If you get frustrated over nothing, things are only going to get worse. No one will feel safe. No one will be able to grow in that environment. Create a space around you where people can feel safe and know there is grace so they can feel safe to grow and change for the better. Implementing that throughout the world is important. I know because I have been on both sides of the coin, both having and not having that safety.

There are more things to be learned and implemented. I'm definitely open to learning as well. I know the main thing for me is meditation. Meditation includes prayer, exercising, chanting, gratitude, visualization, and intense focus. Meditation is slowing down your racing thoughts that may overwhelm you, taking care of your mind, putting yourself into a positive state, and focusing. What you focus on expands.

We can see that through our own lives. Each of us wrote our own stories. Wherever you are, you decided to be there. Yes, circumstances vary, and we come from different situations, but you could always choose to do things differently and write your future a new way. Life is based on decisions and choices. We get to decide where we want to go and our direction to get there. We have to choose. We can think from a place of abundance or a place of scarcity. It is important to take our time and realize how fortunate and how powerful we are. We are great people that can help many others, if we are willing to grow and learn.

Be. Do. Have. We have to make sure we are in the right state of mind as we go down our paths. I believe that your results aren't as great when you don't make sure that, as you journey toward success, you are a good person as well. If you are successful in wealth or some endeavor, but you are not being a good person and doing the right things to get there, the success is tainted and will crumble.

When I started building my financial independence business, I realized that in order to do so, I had to build a team. I started learning even more because I was building a big business. It made my mind expand and think bigger, just like that guy's shirt during the meditation retreat that read, "Be more legendary." Both helped me think bigger and see a way to unite society, raise distribution for great products, and connect people. I will need partners that will be able to broaden our work in agriculture once we reach that point and help us reduce meat consumption. I see how we can prosper. As we prosper, we will continually think even more about how to help the world.

We will be able to connect with people in a higher economic class. We will give them somewhere to direct their charity and generosity, and they will invest in the necessary causes and resources. The people we work with will have great hearts because the only way to succeed with what we do is to serve people. The only way you can serve people is if you grow yourself because this business is not one where you can just go sign people up or tell them what to do; we are all partners.

You have to grow yourself so you can help lead other people, following John C. Maxwell's *Five Levels of Leadership*. We're leaders of leaders. We help other people become leaders. That's how we grow our wealth: by helping people be better versions of themselves and teach them how to extend their love to more people. To me, that's the most beautiful thing. We're helping people in their relationships, which are the most important thing in the world. We're helping them with their health, their finances, and everything, all from one simple business platform.

If I am going to work with others to lead the world in the right direction, my heart has to be purified. To make money and help others succeed, I have to be pure at heart. It's not about me anymore. To continue to grow in my business and to serve people at a higher level, I have to grow as a person, become better, nicer, more loving, and stronger, and have more integrity. It is such a beautiful thing.

Do unto others as you would have done to yourself, the golden rule. I had to learn to think from other people's perspectives in order to be able to push them forward. I had to slow down with people and continue to be aggressive in my own work ethic.

I wanted to be a doctor when I was younger. Now, I'm healing people with the biggest things, finances and positivity, which is going to decrease stress, a leading cause of death. I'm taking care of everything the way I always wanted to take care of it.

Stand in your vision and do what it takes to have it turn out. It does not have to be exactly as you planned it, as long as the vision comes to fruition.

First comes the mind. That's what this business works on. I'm realizing more and more how important people are, and Body, Mind, and Soul is another avenue to serve people globally who are not in the business.

In the financial independence business, we teach people how to eat healthy through their own business.

I am going down a better path for my life. I'm not sure what's right for your life, but for me, this is where I need to be. I am seeing a way to create great wealth while working with others to help them create wealth as well.

I love this because it is not a pyramid. Traditional jobs are where one person has more advantage than the other people, the person on the top always makes the most. Here, whoever is willing to do the work and puts in the time, effort, and energy can succeed.

What we are doing is multifaceted. Everything leads up to the bigger picture of world peace, joining people together, working to end suffering, making sure everyone has food, water, shelter, and clothing, furthering our work to holistic healthcare and education. In our vision, we inspire and love one another, especially the young and unmotivated. This will keep us all on a level playing field, so people don't have to suffer to such extremes. People are starving while there's so much food in this world. People don't have clothes while there is so much material out there. People can't shower when there's so much good water and science to clean the water. That's the real focus, and that's where we are headed.

How will I develop myself to help this vision come to fruition? What am I going to do in the next few years? What are we going to implement in this world peace project to make sure that it grows to be successful? What is it going to take? What is the vision? How are we going to create these systems to establish a level playing field where everybody is good and has enough sustenance?

We will continue to elevate toward the right things and heal our planet and its people.

TRANSITIONS AND GROWTH

Committing is the hard part. Well, committing can be easy. Following through is the hardest part because your emotions get involved. Why am I getting up at four in the morning, right? We forget why. We say we don't have enough time that the body needs rest. We say, "I am sleepy" and "I don't know if this is healthy." We ask, "Why do I push myself so hard?" We say, "You are doing enough. Give yourself some grace."

I agree. Don't beat yourself up. Why not push yourself? Why not do as much as you can? Why not seize every day? Why not become your best? Why not be your strongest self?

Face your challenges and take them head-on. You know what you need to do. You need time.

If you have to get up earlier for you to have more time, do it. We need to—it is not a "get to" conversation—develop personally and spiritually. When I say develop personally, I don't mean the core habits of reading and listening to audios, which is necessary as well. It's very important for you to take care of your health, eat clean, and exercise. You need to exercise because it boosts your self-confidence. It keeps you in the right mindset. Listen to motivational things and meditate so you can slow down and come to compassion. And pray so you can release to a higher power, give thanks, have understanding, and relieve your anxiety.

We need to stay focused on where we want to go. Visualize and guide your thoughts, especially from your runaway nonsensical thoughts. Focus on where you are headed and your goals.

It is important to train our mind because it doesn't know the difference between reality and fantasy. We need to visualize where we want to go. Mentally rehearse things if you need to. We have to slow down in the morning to prepare for the day. We have to slow down at night to reflect, get better sleep, and prepare for the next day.

I had to ask myself, "What is the biggest struggle we have, Jay?" The answer was laziness. The bed is so comfortable. But how comfortable would it be if that was where I was going to be for the rest of my life? In that same place? How will you move forward? By getting to the next level. Life doesn't get easier, but life gets better if you stay consistent in the right habits, such as building health and wealth, and keep growing.

What is that next level going to be like? Will it be a little upgrade? Or is it going to be a dramatic change? Is it going to be life-altering? Is it going to change your whole family's wealth for generations? Are you going to create that impact for the world? Will you inspire them?

Or are you just going to move up to a mediocre level in a mediocre way?

That's the difference between getting up early and getting up when you're rested.

Not saying you don't need rest. If you meditate, reflect, and plan the night before, you can set up a plan and attack that plan. Your mind and God (or your higher power) will give you the energy. When you are prepared, you can achieve much more.

You won't be tired. You won't feel overwhelmed. You'll be in the right space.

Instead of being underwhelmed or overwhelmed and spending your time on nonsense, why don't you take care of yourself? When you're not in the right space, your mind goes so berserk that you don't do what you're truly capable of doing.

Your morning and night routines are very important, Jay. They're among the most important things for you to maintain. Remember that three months of accomplishments at the beginning of the business were due to the fact that you stayed with your routines and kept your spirituality high.

Another key thing is not eating past a certain hour unless you are out with people or at an event. Even then, you want to make sure you eat lightly at night.

On a regular day, you should never catch yourself eating late at night. Drink some more water and head to bed. If you struggle with taking your multivitamins, take them earlier if you need to. Plan ahead.

Work that plan. You can even plan when you're going to eat. It stops you from eating sporadically, filling time gaps in your day by snacking. Because you are thinking so much, you end up defaulting to eating, so you don't have to think. Slow down if you need to. Give yourself a break. I am not saying a two- or three-hour break. It can be brief.

Take a moment for meditation. Take a walk. Do what you need to do to keep your mind focused. Work on all your goals physically, spiritually, emotionally, and mentally.

We know and need to be mindful of how our choices have taken a toll on our lives in the past. Our habits can make us or break us.

Which habits are we going to choose?

Think about it. What's going to spread the most love among everyone? We know you need to meditate and be one with the world so that you can come to that compassion, peace, love, and unity. Same thing with prayer and releasing to a high power. Realize that those choices matter and that we all play a functional role in the bigger picture of this world.

Our life is based on our choices and decisions.

Those temporary decisions become permanent lifestyles. What kind of lifestyle do you want?

Do you want mediocrity? Do you want just above average? Or do you want to live an extraordinary life that allows you to bless and help tons of people?

Think about the word "extraordinary." It means more than the ordinary.

Do a little extra than the ordinary and become extraordinary.

The next transition I want you to make, Jay, is to hit that alarm for 4:00 a.m., 5:00 a.m. at the latest. Be wise; get at least three to four hours of sleep. You could take naps during the day if you need to. Stick with one time because if you say 5:00 a.m. at the latest, it ends up being 6:00 a.m. because you never decided. Then you beat yourself up for getting up at five because you should have gotten up earlier, so just get up. The only way you're going to get up is if you figure out a way to get off the bed and sit up. Don't let getting back on the bed be an option. The only way, Jay, is to put your alarm further away from you. Before you turn off that alarm, make up the bed so you can't go back to it.

If you get up and lay on the yoga mat, you will be stretching and getting your mind right. You know you cannot sleep that long on the yoga mat. It's going to relax you. It is going to do everything you need it to do. Solution found.

Wake up.

Smile. Be thankful for life.

Think about how magnificent your life is going to be and how amazing the day ahead of you will be.

Breathe. Drink some water.

Go exercise, visualize, meditate, chant, and eat.

Get yourself prepared. Journal, plan your day, and review your schedule.

And don't fill your day so much that you can't be present in your life and have to rush around all the time. Being busy doesn't mean you're becoming successful.

You want to be organized and planned. You want to plan and execute. It doesn't have to be so strenuous. Be efficient. Look at the long term, focus on the short term, let go, and let God. Don't try to control every situation. All you can do is show up. Be unoffendable. Be loving and be caring. Being loving allows you to lead people, so you can help them to the right decision for them or the decision that will impact their lives positively. Do what you say you're going to do, no matter what. Whether somebody is there or not, follow through.

Meditation and reflection helped me connect with the earth. My mindset was more abundant. I was able to realize how much of everything I needed was there already instead of living in fear that we wouldn't have enough. It allowed me to heal my past hurts, forgive others and myself, and stay focused on the future and where I was headed.

I was able to work with my family so we could cultivate even more blessings and work on growing ourselves. Sometimes you have to free yourself to free others.

If you choose not to be free, how many others may suffer?

Maybe sometimes helping yourself and setting up the bigger picture is the best thing you can do.

You are responsible for helping everybody in your life live a better life, if they will allow you to help. Be responsible. Make sure you are helping them get what they want and are not just selling them a mansion, giving them what *you* want to give them without finding out what they want or need.

We all have decisions to make. For example, one time, my father wanted salt but told me he didn't want me to get it for him because we had an argument. He said to let Trisha go get it for him, and she took $35 from his EBT card. She paid him back after she initially denied it. That would have never happened if I took responsibility and did what I had to do as the holder of his card.

We are responsible for all things within our control. That's a little example, but it is as simple as that.

My father lost his money and lost his medicinal marijuana because I didn't put it in the drawer, thinking he would do it. I should not have left it up to him. That's what I mean by you being responsible for everything in your life. I couldn't care less about the weed. My goal was to help him pay his way to Trinidad.

Another incident is I didn't go with my family to go get the first car. They ended up getting jipped. It wasn't that bad, but I could have helped them. They opened the door for me to help, but sometimes I don't want to take the time unless I am asked directly for help. I don't always take the initiative and do not want to be responsible for things going wrong.

Be responsible for everything in your life.

You get it? Everything.

I questioned myself about one of my business partners not succeeding in the business. Did I build a strong enough relationship with him, so he would feel empowered? Did I do enough for him to realize that I loved and cared for him? I wanted him to grow with us and know that he is important to me.

Did I do that? Did I do enough? Am I doing enough?

Yeah, it felt like a lot of work. I felt like I was pushing myself and doing a lot.

But I wondered, "Can I do more, in a disciplined and joyful manner?"

That's why it's very important to take care of my mind. Be at ease. Be full of love, compassion, and understanding. It helps you to be able to take care of others.

That is cultivated. That doesn't happen without work. Sure, you can be a genuinely good person. You still need time for yourself. Get up to take time for yourself so you can be optimal throughout your day.

Plan some downtime with the family, with your partner, and for yourself. Don't let business get in the way of those things. Don't let anything get in the way. Those things are going to fill up your love tank and your soul. That will help you prosper, perform even better, and work harder for what you really want.

You are doing great.

Remember, meditation helped me get As while I was working full-time. I ended up leaving my job and still getting money because I started getting scholarships. I received an emerging scholar award. I did research, and I got paid for it. Meditation opened up a lot of doors for me.

Why was that? Because you think abundantly when you slow down your thoughts. I didn't have to study as much because I slowed down and meditated after every study session. All of these things add up. It may seem like meditation is taking up time, but those precious moments spent praying or meditating will elevate you a lot quicker than just doing the work.

Don't get me wrong; you have to do the work if you want the results.

You have to allow the blessings in. Ask, believe, and receive. I feel like if you ask for a lot, you will have to work a lot, but if you do not take the time to relax and revive and cultivate your mind into a positive state, especially when you are working diligently, your belief will diminish.

I was one of the few kids to get an A in organic chemistry because I meditated and studied.

While researching and developing myself during my classes at college, I continued my meditation. I took off meditation for a portion of a year because of the vibration I had felt. I had heard about astral travel and got scared. I started doing more drugs at that time in my life because I needed to slow down and drugs slowed me down. I smoked a lot of weed.

When I started meditating, I earned a 4.0 GPA, but I wasn't taking care of my health. I was still smoking and drinking on the weekends. I was getting chubbier, and that all takes a toll on your energy, your mind, and your self-confidence. Lack of self-confidence leads to jealousy.

Then I was taking an EMT course in addition to sixteen credits at school. These were hard classes such as biochemistry, biophysical chemistry, analytical chemistry, and intensive Spanish. I was really pushing myself to the limit.

I was volunteering and growing myself as much as possible.

I started working out that summer and never really stopped working out after that. That was when I was coming out of my first relationship. I was giving up the habits of smoking and drinking. I cut back drastically on smoking. Drinking was more of a social thing. I never really drank alone, except for once or twice when I was pre-gaming by myself before going to a party. Later on, I used it for good times instead of using it to forget everything. I had better times when I didn't use it at all, though. I didn't realize that until much later.

Meditation led me to being able to volunteer, work out, relieve pain from my ex-girlfriend, earn a 3.8 GPA, complete sixteen class credits, work a job, and become a leader in my fraternity, all because I was able to organize my thoughts, be calm, and cultivate good energy. This also helped me with time management. I learned not to repeat thoughts as much, reducing my stress level, so I can retain more knowledge.

My life was not a straight shot. It had a lot of crisscrosses and winding roads, but I was more focused and task- and goal-oriented and got things done instead of being stuck in my mind and my thoughts. If I didn't slow down, I probably would not have thought of this book, how it is going to help the world, or how I was going to cultivate these things. In addition, I now have the blessings of my family. They are always pushing me to do better, even if they were mean at times, which was not the right motivation. Sometimes, you need that vibration to snap you out of it and wake you up.

The following year, I worked in real estate after studying for the MCAT. I didn't really want to be in school for the next four years. For two years, I had a lot of fun with girls to boost my ego. I wanted to feel more secure with women if I was ever to get married. I was still hurt from my first girlfriend. I got very good at being with women.

I became a real estate agent because I wanted to make money while I was an EMT, sleeping two to three hours a night. I still closed a few deals when people weren't closing any deals. I could have closed a lot more deals if I got more sleep. It was not about sleep but rather doing the work to reduce the fear. Fear holds you back. It creates anxiety. The more I meditated and worked out, the clearer my mind became and the more I executed.

I didn't want to get too fatigued because you can get fatigued, do nothing, and harm yourself. But you could push yourself and do more than you ever thought you could. When I got into real estate, I did public speaking at Toastmasters. I was also reflecting on my life and journaling. It was especially helpful when I started the year of real estate and needed to overcome my past and look in the mirror to become better and more disciplined.

I cut off all the women.

I woke up by doing more professional and personal development and cleaning up my mind.

Before my shifts in real estate work, I began meditating again and getting over the traumas of my own mind, exhaustion, self-pity, and depression.

I could not see the blessings that I was opening myself up to, but I could see the path that I was closing off. I never closed it off, though. I took a different direction to lead to more abundance and a different purpose. After writing down my purpose, my vision and mindset grew to make it happen.

I was fighting my growing purpose at times. I felt I was doing the wrong thing. Sometimes you have to listen to your intuition and just believe. When my path was shifting, many tribulations came about. It was very hard to believe that God/I created this clear path for me to be a doctor. Now I'm shifting to a new path, and I'm not saying it's not more abundant or beautiful. I need to start looking at my end goals and stop looking at short-term pleasures.

It was the belief factor that made the difference because I did all that work to become a doctor. My belief was firm in that area. I knew I could do those things because I did the work. The more you do the work, the more your belief grows. The more phone calls I made about real estate, the more my belief went up. The more I talked to people and followed up and followed through, which I need to be doing with my financial independence business as I think about it, the more things came together. I have to believe and do the work, continually increasing my capacity. I can do more. I could always follow up a lot better. I have to track my business again. When I started tracking, I realized I was not doing as much as I thought I was doing. I'm going to kill this. I'm going to do so well.

My success was possible because of the routines I have set up, including spirituality and business practices daily and nightly. These routines are the most important thing. You have to set up routines, change them, adapt them, and make them work to help you get the results you need. Follow through with them. Don't downplay them and act like they're not doing anything for you. They do so much, you just can't see easily because you're looking at the day-to-day actions. You have to look at the bigger picture. Are you actually blowing people and your goals out of the water but can't even see it? Look at your long-term vision; it reduces the emotional ups and downs of the day-to-day.

A successful man in our industry said not to underestimate the work of a day because it adds up to the week, weeks to the month, months to the year, then to two and five years—to ten years. It all adds up. If you don't see the results in a day or two, it is okay because the big picture is what matters. Do the work, follow through, and enjoy the process. The results will come.

Before shifting and starting to make the calls, I dropped all my good habits. That is how my first book came about, from my first feeling of depression in my life. I stopped working out, meditating, and eating right.

When I came home from work, I scrolled social media and used pornography to try to sleep. I did that for two weeks. Getting off track for two weeks was enough to make me have suicidal thoughts. It was only one thought, but it was a strong thought. It was a powerful vibration. Imagine you live a decent life. You have all the options in the world. You can build your own life. You didn't always have the best surroundings or circumstances, but you had a safe haven. You had your sanctuary. You had your safe place. A lot of people didn't have that, but you had yours. What happened next?

I was lying in my bed, and a thought came into my head.

"Jay, if life is so bad, why don't you jump out the window? Just open the window and jump out."

I was like, "What?"

And the voice said, "Yeah, open the window and jump out."

And then I got up.

I shook it off. Slowly, I had to clear the cobwebs. I started practicing my meditation, daily affirmations, and getting more consistent with mindfulness. Going through the self-development path, knocking out the nonsense, and believing again helped me turn over a new leaf and get on this new path.

I started back on my journey.

I started doing transcendental meditation.

I got back into cultivating my meditation at Dharma Path CUNY by teaching others and made my own meditation even stronger. I was still struggling at that time because I was doing so much, volunteering at Toastmasters, holding two major roles. I could have done a better job, even though I got an award while there. I could have made it to the President's Distinguished Club.

You can always succeed.

But at what level do you want to succeed? That's what you have to determine. And you have to put in the work behind it. I picked up my wellness practices again to stay focused and on task and resumed bullet journaling.

I was just getting things done. My life was transitioning. I did all the things I intended to do. I closed a real estate transaction and completed my ninety-day leadership journey. I met my girl, had a perfect moment with my mom, wrote the book, and so much more.

I started doing a free public meditation call in the morning. I did this for sixty-seven days straight. Those sixty-seven days were part of the three-month journey. Meditation helped me start Body, Mind, and Soul, which will grow globally, and that pushed me to do everything I wanted.

I became fitter and am currently living a vegan lifestyle. I wake up with more compassion and love and try to maintain my healthy habits and be committed to my word. Each of those sixty-seven days, I got up at 5:00 a.m., meditated, did my call, and worked out, plus my core habits.

I lost $100 throwing our retreat in the Dominican Republic during that journey, but I still managed to go on the trip and cover travel, food, and lodging for my girl, her mother, and me. But I always remind myself of how much I learned and how much I gained.

The experience, giving my girl's mama a vacation while learning so many skills together, was priceless. I learned how creative my mind was. In those three months, I had over twenty speaking engagements, established an LLC, and became a life coach. I spoke in schools, got a vendor's license, and created a curriculum to speak in those schools. I read an award-winning book on connecting and leading, created an awesome email template, and learned how to connect with people and grow both of my businesses, all in three months.

Why? Because I got up and I made the time to cultivate my mind. I stayed organized, and I got things done. So don't stop and do that for the next four to five years. Get up and get what you need done. It doesn't take you that long. You have the skills and can absolutely do this. Build yourself so we can transform this world. Let's get the results.

Let's work out. Let's get fit. Let's get our finances together. Let's do what we need to do.

I love you to death.

Now we're going to show what the future will look like. We will visualize and bring it to fruition. The words that come in the next chapters come from love, grace, generosity, and God's Word through me. I devote myself and surrender to the higher power for the betterment of this world. To create something bigger than myself, for my family, for my friends, for the world, for the universe, for my ancestors who have passed, and for all celestial beings. We will impact this world. It only takes one man to change the world. You do need a team, though. You can't do everything by yourself.

But you have to start with you.

World peace starts within every one of us. Peace starts inside of you.

This mission begins with you.

Let's go.

THE IDEAL VISION

Everything happens for a reason.

I was reading a quote the other day on a social media page, stating that there is a season for everything. A pastor in our business talks about it too. I went to the personal development program and made a contract with myself that says, "I am a humble, urgent, giving leader."

I see through time how that is coming to fruition.

I used to beat myself up. If I didn't get up on time or did any little thing wrong, I would beat myself up. Sometimes I don't even hear my alarm.

I realized God was putting me through these tests.

I feel the lesson is to be humble, even with myself. How I treat myself is how I may treat others.

That's my contract. I'm a humble, urgent, giving leader. The first declaration is that I'm humble.

I think the reason is to make sure I have grace for people. Don't judge people. Allow them to have that safe environment to grow.

The business is teaching me that and leadership skills. I'm becoming humbler and working to live in my contract as I continue to develop myself.

I'm moving toward greater things. Let's move on to the vision.

Think less and do more. Make sure you give yourself space to continuously improve and have time to reflect on and remember the highlights and lessons of the day.

Where are we headed?

We are headed to a beautiful place. We're going to take care of many things on this path.

This is the journey I'm going through with my contract. I'm humble, but can you even be humble when you say you are humble?

I had to become a little bit selfish and work on myself so I could become humbler. Being humble to me is being respectful and kind to everyone.

I am in an urgent stage in my life. I will continue being humble and build on top of each foundational level. Urgency will be ineffective if I am forgetting to be humble along the way. Now I can move with more efficiency. I have less angst. I know where I'm headed. I know the business works. I know what I'm doing, yet I am still learning. I believe in myself and my business. I have faith. I see results due to my effort and work.

I built my relationship with God and the higher power. I want to continue to maintain and deepen that connection. As I grow myself, I have more and more successes in the things that I do.

My giving is growing abundantly. I give in all that I do.

I'm giving God my all. I also feel being urgent involves diligence, hard work, and discipline (while remaining humble).

Don't let the hard work phase you, change you as a person, or frustrate you while you're doing so many new and different things. Always be loving and giving. If you can't, slow down. Maybe you're doing too much.

It's about being humble, urgent, and then add on giving.

I am a humble, urgent, giving leader.

I've been writing down goals for a while. Business goals, life goals, this book, and other things. I've been hitting my goals at about 30 percent of my potential because of my focus. No one is perfect. I have to keep recalibrating and become more disciplined. I am working to create the right habits. Your habits will give you the life you want.

My business comes after my relationship with God. I know this will help me blossom the most as a person. It keeps me focused because of the core steps. The work allows me to develop my mind every day, stay on track, and keep consistent with my positive habits. My relationship with God is one thing, but I must also prioritize my spirituality for the maximum effect. This includes meditation, prayer, gratitude, visualization, and positive affirmations. You can test it yourself: sit up, practice gratitude, chant some positive affirmations, visualize the life you want to create, pray, and meditate. See how that helps you.

That is where my self-development journey is at the moment.

It's beautiful. I'm adding on to my routines and rituals, and I am finding new ways to implement them and trying not to lose them by becoming lazy. I'm learning how to work through my environment, my surroundings, and my excuses.

I have my big why and my purpose.

I have to see the things that may hold me back and the things that keep me on track. The things that may hold me back include not maintaining a peaceful, conducive work environment and putting myself in situations where I could be lazy, like lying down in my bed, reading, and falling asleep when I could be working. The new habits are sinking in. As I work harder, I learn how to use them to my benefit. As my desire to be more efficient and increase my capacity grows, I learn more about how to be my best self.

Where are we headed?

I'm going to perfect my body. I'm going to work on myself and on my health and gain strength through the business. I keep saying through the business, but the real growth happens when I increase my spirituality because faith plus work equals success. I need to keep my spirituality high and do the work. My work involves taking care of my health and funding my business all while I am working on myself, exercising five to six (if not seven) times a week, in a peaceful, rhythmic way. The goal is to do this, getting maximum results, while not stressing my body.

This also means pushing myself yet plotting time for having fun. I can do things like riding my bike and writing my story. It's about enjoying life while working hard at living the best life, a fulfilling life, and seizing every moment. I'm growing stronger, taking in more positive information, and learning how we can move forward in the direction we need to move.

Where are we headed? I keep asking this, right?

We are headed toward world peace. How do you get there?

By growing Body, Mind, and Soul and our financial independence business.

By waking up the world on how we can heal the planet instead of destroying it.

By exploring how we can heal one another through loving one another, working together, and creating positive environments for change.

Every day, as I grow in my businesses and connections, doing whatever it takes, I grow and become a stronger me. Body, Mind, and Soul is going to wake up a lot of people. Our financial freedom work will also wake up people and give them a financial incentive to become better human beings.

For instance, police are great people. They sacrifice their lives for us. I love them. A lot of my friends are officers, and I thank them so much for serving. I've been an EMT, and I've seen the nonsense cops have to deal with. Cops are here to make sure we are protected as a society. Cops try to help people. Even when people are doing the wrong things, cops still try to give them the benefit of the doubt. When your life is threatened, and you just want to get home to your kids, would you play around?

What would you do?

Cops are taught to stereotype, though, when in certain areas checking out certain demographics. It makes sense. If your pants are low and you are acting like a thug, I would watch you too. It happens to people who have tattoos in some Asian communities where people may judge them, thinking they are a triad or a gang member.

Honestly, crookedness starts from the top and trickles down. That's the reason we would want to get to the top so we could change everything for the better and have power to inspire more people to live a more wholesome life. How could we create good leaders? With the right leadership training.

What I wonder in regard to cops is whether we can eradicate weapons. Can we do away with them? Will cops be safe? Are weapons necessary in society?

We have to figure that out.

Maybe we could even put locks on guns that require fingerprint recognition for the gun to work.

I believe all officers should be very well trained in some form of martial arts. Their gun should be the last resort. They should be confident enough within themselves and strong enough with their work ethic and health that they won't need to pull out a gun in these situations. They will be confident, respectful, and loving to everyone, no matter what stereotype someone fits in. We all treat everyone with respect, love, and give them the benefit of the doubt.

Meditation and prayer will also increase their focus so they will be aware and alert, enabling them to handle situations more efficiently and cultivate their inner peace. When you are at peace, you actually see more clearly, which would increase your awareness, ultimately increasing your chances of survival.

Even if certain people have been known to be notoriously bad, we are not allowing them to change if we keep judging them based on their past. Believing in them and motivating them will allow them to become better.

This is what we teach around bullying in Body, Mind, and Soul.

People are not bullies. We don't define someone as a bully or a victim. Bullying is an action, and so is acting like a victim.

We can act in a victimized way and actively bully others. We don't say, "He is a bully" or "She's a bully," because we are only classifying people in that direction. You have given them that identification, but that's not who they are; they are human beings.

We have to learn to love everybody and give them the grace to be able to change.

Let them define themselves by their actions. We should remember we are all human beings, we are all a work of art. See the greatness in people and focus on that. Allow that to grow. Help them pull their greatness out. What you get attention for is what you express. Build on that.

When we say, "Oh, he's bad because he is a bully" or "She's good because she does her homework," both have an impact. What you focus on expands. If I say that you're bad, now you're more likely to classify yourself as bad, cut school, do drugs, and hang out with gangs because they accept you, and we categorize those activities as what someone who is bad would do.

Now if I say you are good when you go study, you may go on to college or do things associated with activities someone who is good would do. Maybe you will become a pushover at your own job, in your classes, or in your life because you are "good" and want to please others.

How about we classify everybody as a human being and learn to live with love and grace, building people with strong morals and ethics? We can all grow in the right direction in a positive, loving, strong, and united environment.

How about having more positive things in society at a more affordable rate? When and how are governments initiating these things? We spend money on drugs, medication, and war instead of spending money to eradicate poverty and starvation and work on creating systems to generate peace, harmony, unity, and love.

What about healing people? What about having community centers where people can go exercise and connect with one another? Maybe even passes for people who are in financial distress or other situations.

Next comes infrastructure. This comes into play via smart cities and having technology work through everything. I feel this is where a point system could work. Everybody should have a select number of points to start with. We would have to develop that process on the back end.

Our business systems can function through a credit or point system, and each action we perform correlates to a certain amount of points.

If you are creative—which includes creating systems, ideas, innovations, and tools for efficiency—or do care work, such as medical and holistic healthcare, because most jobs are going to be eradicated eventually, you would acquire more points for the tasks you perform. You will still be able to have more luxuries of life, depending on your work ethic.

This would be a capitalist society, where everybody has a bare minimum, which is a better standard than we have right now. It would be a society where everyone has somewhere to sleep, a nice home, clean clothes, and food, yet we would still have the ability to build, to keep innovation and thriving systems alive.

When you work in creativity and care fields, you can earn more points. We want to continue with innovation and forward motion. We have to eradicate a lot of things and help companies transition, so there is no big uproar or chaos, or they will get left behind. Before we talk about eradicating stuff, let's talk about building a strong team.

I became focused and healthy and grew myself. I am intellectual yet down-to-earth and loving. Everybody likes to be around me. I worked to create a safe environment for everybody to feel loved and respected.

The team has grown into the thousands. We have created all the major events across the northeast. As leaders, we could create remarkable changes in this world, change for the betterment of all communities.

We could eradicate mass meat production, which will affect a lot of pharmaceutical companies and meat companies.

Why won't the meat companies be on board now?

We must start the mass meat production decline, transition over, and learn how to make more vegan products more accessible. It is going to heal the planet. We will work and figure that out. Once we shift and stop mass meat production, we can reduce carbon dioxide emissions. Then the ozone layer can be healed instead of being destroyed to the extreme where people are getting sunburned creating cancer.

The Arctic is dissolving. When we graze the seventy billion animals that we produce yearly and cut down fields and forests, these animals let out carbon dioxide, and we do not have resources such as trees to absorb that carbon dioxide. We are creating a double effect on carbon dioxide emissions, not including the methane and fecal matter that we cannot get rid of fast enough. The fecal matter and urine are sprayed with hoses into surrounding neighborhoods to remove the waste when they cannot dispose of them promptly enough. This practice is detrimental and creates hypertension, asthma, and so many other diseases within the surrounding, usually impoverished, population. The waste fields are sometimes the size of four football fields for one farm.

We allow the planet to heal by having more plants and vegetation. We go to places that are run-down and desolate; instead of treating them like a nuisance, we make them a contribution. We grow people, their talents, and the land's resources. We increase agriculture and make usable land.

The government can make money from this. We are not going to stop the government from making money off of it. We will give the government profits. It's not about taking but about healing the people, the communities, and the planet.

If the government wants some funds, they can have it, as long as we have enough to sustain growth and heal the earth. We grow more vegetation and we increase the number of schools, so while the parents are working, the kids have somewhere to go.

We will create wellness centers. So it's not about waiting until you get sick; you have somewhere that is a safe environment to heal mentally, physically, emotionally, and spiritually. Being proactive in that way will keep you healthy in all areas. Eventually, we will create a TV channel where people can surf and learn how to practice gratitude and positive affirmations. It will help them reform their minds to positivity by focusing on all that they have, creating an abundant mindset.

We have reached as a world to such peace and unity growing in strength.

We would even approach the warriors and people who are causing wars and figure out what the root cause is. Once we figure it out, we will have figured out how to remove the chance of future conflict.

The whole wellness system will be changed. Medicine will still be prevalent, but preventative care will be the main source of care, including holistic, natural healing. We won't treat symptoms; we will treat the whole person, the whole being.

Doctors must have time to talk and get a holistic view of the person, but society has made them rush. They became doctors to do something good with their lives, but due to protocols and insurance policies, they can't even do what's best for people anymore.

We will eradicate violence, gangs, stereotyping and categorizing people, and continue working toward helping people heal.

How? With wellness centers, television stations, unification games, and education on how to treat others.

I'm so passionate about stopping mass meat production because I've seen the things that happen to get meat to tables. I've created a documentary on this before. It showed me how much we were destroying the planet, with the massive fields of animal urine and waste, as well as the land destroyed for the hundreds of millions of animals we produce annually to have space to graze.

And we have to give these animals so much water, food, and other resources.

Just because we want the luxury of having meat.

It is not even necessary for a diet. I don't think anything is wrong with meat. The problem is we consume too much of it. We have to be more moderate in our consumption and in what we do.

People are starving, and the amount of food we give these animals could feed the world twice.

What really woke me up?

What woke me up was a thirteen-year-old girl that was on social media preaching to the government, saying if you don't know how to fix our planet, at least don't destroy it. We, as adults, are older and supposedly wiser. We could heal the planet. We have the rights, choices, and means to do it. We have to bond together and heal the planet for the future. We could all live well. There's so much abundance on this planet. Why fight it? Let's use technology and start implementing systems for world peace.

Let's mass-produce things that are going to heal the planet and make life more efficient, so we could enjoy time with our friends and family. In schools, we should teach good things, topics that are high in morality and wholeness that will really change our society in a dramatic way.

In the world, we want to work on solar projects, agriculture, and building homes, schools, and holistic centers so communities can grow from poverty to contribution.

The school system should teach life lessons, like how to manage the household, how to cook and fend for ourselves, job functions, how to deal with issues, how to treat one another, how to treat and grow ourselves, and whatever needs to be done.

With some work, diseases can be eradicated, along with the reduction of pesticides and hormones that produce animals for mass production. In this world, people have enough and feel abundant, which includes trusting and loving one another, spreading good energy.

Once mass meat production is done, the planet will be able to breathe again. In this future, I envision that we eat healthy and optimally and our mindsets are changing. We feel and operate out of positivity instead of feeling heavy and drained of energy from treating our stomachs like cemeteries, filling our bodies with carcasses, and treating others poorly. (That cycle makes people want to be in an actual cemetery and be sedentary and sleep.)

How do we do this again?

This is the overview.

Let's zoom in. This is what I see:

We're in Spokane, Washington.

We are at a life-changing event, a family reunion. I just engaged my fiancée on an airplane on the day of our anniversary.

She is a flight attendant. I promise her we don't need to fly on standby anymore. We are going to live a great life. Our belief is growing. My work ethic is growing, and my bond with God is being strengthened. Everything is going to change for the better because I'm willing to work for it. My desire has increased so much.

I love people so much more.

Our team is growing. My body is changing. I'm becoming better, stronger, and smarter every day. I'm working, reading, taking time to enjoy the days spent with my family and friends, and having a magnificent life. We are having barbecues and chilling while our business is growing tenfold within the next year. Body, Mind, and Soul is growing rapidly. I'm making six figures off that business, talking at corporations and schools, making BMS into a huge corporation. We get to a point where we have to hire somebody to be the CEO and run it as we switch it into a nonprofit, reducing our personal activity down to a minimum.

We hire the right person that believes in the vision, to help us manifest it, and transition into a nonprofit, so it can receive grants and offer more free services to the public. We expand to open our wellness centers, where everyone benefits and everybody who works there is treated and paid well.

Over time, we change all of society, including the healthcare and education systems, by showing people how to meditate in a way that resonates with them, grow their mindset, harness creativity, and perform artistic tasks. Medicine is necessary. We do need it for when people get injured or need surgery. The key is to heal people holistically and not only treat symptoms.

We learn to cleanse people's minds and bring them to peace, allowing them to heal themselves. Our businesses are growing. We are becoming better speakers, better motivators, and greater at connecting and communicating with people.

We sit down with the leaders of industries and institutions.

Our book is endorsed by many people with great influence. The book will reach the top of many charts and lists, and the movie is about to come out.

Our life is changing dramatically.

We finally get married. It is a beautiful marriage.

The wedding is magnificent. We dance and put on a performance. Our relationships grow richer. I have someone taking care of my father again.

I am helping him even more because now he's motivated to do the right things.

My mom will retire from her job in the next year. We have more than enough income to retire both of our parents. They get to go to Grenada or wherever they want, whenever they want. Our business is growing massively. We end up having some of the highest percentages of the global volume of our business. We start working with the right people to create world peace, and our nonprofit comes to fruition.

Body, Mind, and Soul is taking care of the police officers, helping them lead better by teaching holistic healing methods, confidence, martial arts, and whatever they need to lead a more peaceful nation. The only way we're going to have world peace is if we have internal peace within ourselves. Peace, to me, comes with confidence, especially needed if you have a job where you're putting your life on the line every day.

This society is in unison, and we are willing to slow down to help one another. Laws have softened and are not so strict. I don't mean the laws of the world, but the rules of jobs and regulations. Jobs are being eradicated, and people are living in better conditions. This is in the next two to five years.

We have grown so much. We are physically fit. The nonprofit is ready. We have targeted locations that have the most poverty. We have identified and partnered with the right companies already doing things needed for world peace. We either collaborate or facilitate and fill in the gaps.

We can also change the world by moving toward solar energy and getting rid of fossil fuels. We would help compensate those who were running businesses involving fossil fuel and aid them in the transition to be more supportive of solar energy. We would help them come on board and transition to the mainstream. They will not have to lose as long as they're willing to learn and grow and support the world in our plan of healing.

Our plan involves finding out where to build the schools and how to promote agriculture and choose whom to work with.

We'll have a massive organization ready to do all of that, with a plan ready to be implemented and a great board full of intellectuals, visionaries, and executives that know how to proceed on these things we discussed.

Our ideas are manifesting. We're making smart cities and healing the planet, and everything is slowly transitioning so everyone can move in grace and not drop down to a low place. Society is able to move in a graceful way. We have some of the most prominent national leaders and world leaders working together to really change the planet. Greed is dissolving slowly.

As I am working on this journey, I will go on amazing trips, full of luxury, in exotic and popular places where we are implementing our world peace plans. We are waking up and walking onto the patio to execute our plans, flying around on our private jet, going to help people in places that are stricken with poverty. Now, we see people with sheds who are getting clothes and supporting the kids in schools, while families are building new homes and using 3D printing. We are making things affordable.

We are eating well, and everybody is living a great lifestyle. We own a massive mansion where we have parties with our friends and family and gatherings with the whole community. In our nineteen-bedroom mansion, we have six or more helpers living comfortably with the ability to build their own lives. We have our parents, and some orphan children live with us as well.

Everybody we know is around us, living their best life, and we are a contribution.

Our movie tops the charts once released and receives amazing reviews.

After the first few weeks of launching the world peace nonprofit, it becomes a billion-dollar organization. Half of the money from the movie pours into the nonprofit.

From the movie revenue, 10 percent goes to us to support our family. Ten to 20 percent will go to the actors, and 20 percent keeps the project running for marketing, expansion, and filling any other gaps. Body, Mind, and Soul is taking care of the health and wellness aspect.

Health and wellness centers are promoting mindfulness, eradicating harm within communities, creating safe environments for people to practice positivity and have access to good activities. That should prevent people from falling into bad things. This means having access to healthy food, sports drinks, health products, and more.

By then, agriculture will have grown so big for us. We have partnered with one of the largest corporations in the world that distributes great produce and products all around the world. People are getting prime produce at affordable prices. This is happening right in front of our eyes, as people are getting stronger in all areas of their lives physically, mentally, spiritually, and emotionally.

We sit still, and everything is manifesting because we're allowing the world to move from a place of chaos to one of unity.

We move from poverty to the Evergreen, to a great, abundant life. We are moving from scarcity to trust and love. People greet and hug each other, work together, and make time to slow down, thus making bigger things happen in life. This is how we become massive and strong as a unit. The world is becoming more beautiful and purer. There are a few dark areas where the government has created turmoil and wars soon to be eradicated.

I become physically fit and have such a great team that we sit down, on the eve of what was to become the Third World War, with the opposition. We are no longer using fossil fuels. We don't need oil as much either. Everybody's coming to a place of peace. Everybody has enough of everything they need. The same areas are not stricken with poverty anymore. We get down to the nitty-gritty with the leaders, both good and bad. We figure out that everybody wants understanding, respect, and love.

We have a meeting with all parties in the conflict. They have their guns; we have ours. I have a vision of flipping the table and going into war and of airports being blown up. We have that vision of the wrong possibilities, like thrown grenades, violent airport takeovers, and launched missiles. As soon as we flip the table, we start killing the terrorists.

Rewinding that future prediction, we come back to sitting at that table. No airports are destroyed. Nothing is destroyed. No shooting happens. All explosions in the world come to a stop.

We all agree to a truce and treaty to work on achieving world peace and establishing systems to improve society.

We agree to allow people to live better lifestyles and all become one with each other, full of love and compassion.

Ultimately, in order to sit down with the opposition, we had to deploy with a few armed men.

We knocked everybody out. We didn't kill one person. We shot them with tranquilizer darts to make them sleep, infiltrated their whole system, captured them, sat them down, and talked. We set up a civil meeting with the terrorist leaders, realizing that none of us wants to go to war. No one wanted to fight. We all needed mutual respect and understanding.

How did we get here, and how will it all end?

BEFORE THE IDEAL VISION

I check in with myself regularly to reflect on where we were in the beginning, the growth journey, what it looks like now, and where we're headed.

I reflect on all the emotional overcoming, the growth in maturity, our strengthened connection with God, and personal and professional growth we've experienced.

What a journey. Life is a blessing. I'm growing in appreciation, gratitude, patience, and leadership skills. I grew stronger when I stopped watching others and started watching myself. Every time I see something wrong with others, I look for it in myself. I look for what I could have done better for my desired outcome. I ask, "How can I be more of a support?"

The more I watch myself for correction, it enables me to offer even more grace and love to others and eliminate judgment. I feel that, in addition to my self-growth, my team is molding me into a diamond. I am learning how to grow and excel in these different situations. My father has taught me so much. He is teaching me not to get offended, how to walk away, and most of all, the connections between how I feel when he hurts me and ways I may be hurting my fiancée. This has helped me treat her better.

My father is facing his own situation. I watch him and ask myself, "How can I help him get better?"

I started hearing the little whispers. My cousin said that when my father went down to Trinidad, we could take him to physical therapy, and I wanted to start taking him the following year. I made it happen right away.

I became more efficient and completed the work I was doing for up to four hours, three days a week, in two hours at most those same three days. I was taking my father to physical therapy appointments. At first, I was helping him in the sessions, but he became very nasty because it was challenging for him. So I let the therapists do their thing, and that gave me more time to learn Spanish, research documentaries, and study other things.

My father's energy was increasing. I was happy for him. His newfound strength led him back to poor decisions. He started smoking more than just weed and cigarettes. When he smokes, he becomes upset with himself and takes it out on the people close to him, including me. I felt his verbal abuse and tantrums were molding me to become unoffendable. He would yell, call me mean names, and talk about my family. Things got to a point where I learned to plug in headphones to drown him out. He would just call me even more names.

That was a challenge, being afraid every time I walked in the house, not knowing whether you were going to meet Jekyll or Hyde. It hurt not being able to talk with my dad, but I turned to more positive habits. I thought I learned how to overcome it, but he was getting more and more abusive. He would do it with Trisha as well, the lady that lives with him. He treated the people closest to him the worst.

One day, I just couldn't take it anymore. When I'm there, I feel compelled to get things done with and for him. I couldn't go back and get him another home aide because he already had negative notes against him on his file. An aide reported him having needles in the home. I kept finding drug paraphernalia there myself.

That day, I said, "Curse at me again, I'll throw water on you." He cursed at me, and I threw water on him. That happened twice, and I realized I let his behavior determine my actions. As I gained more control over myself and my actions, our relationship grew.

He is clinically bipolar and schizophrenic, but from my experiences, his behaviors are decisions, and some people enable them. I gained more self-control and became more unoffendable. He would still push me.

I told him, "You get upset with me because you are choosing to smoke that garbage. You broke up the family thirty years ago over drugs. You yell and put down my cousin for smoking it, but you continue to do it. Wake up!"

I spoke to him from a place of resentment and hurt. We fought over something again. The next day, which was a beautiful day, I met my sister on the train and made two or three contacts for my business. We exchanged good mornings and hellos.

On the way, I said hi to the workers through the glass of the coffee shop as I passed.

I then walked into my pop's home, and he looked stuck. He had a crack pipe in his hand.

He had taken a hit. The smoke was still seeping out. I can remember that moment so vividly. So many emotions washed over me.

That was the first time I actually saw him in the act.

I told the guest that he had, "Let's take a walk." I told my father, "I love you. I'll be back to take you to your physical therapy appointment. Clean yourself up."

I spoke to the guy who was with my father and said that even though it may be my father's decision, you are enabling him with these activities. I wished him the best and told him, "I wouldn't want that for you either."

I went back to the cafe because that was the last place I had felt love and good vibes.

There, I had another shift. I learned to accept people for who they are. I'm working to come from a place of grace and love. I realized how important it is to build people up, show them their importance, and encourage them in the right direction, all things my mentor was very good at doing with me. He would break me down and build me back up.

After physical therapy, I spoke to my pops about being a leader and said that, between him and Trisha, one of them had to be the leader. I told them that they had to work together and pick each other up, to work through this, and to make it out of this.

I felt my leadership coming out. I was building a vision for them and giving them each an important role, encouraging and motivating them in a positive direction.

Many things are growing concurrently: the business, my relationships with my mentor and my friends and family, my knowledge of leaders, and the clarity around directions I need to take for the nonprofit and BMS. I am still working on listening to God. I would focus on financial independence solely, but I feel God is telling me to write this book, and that this story and vision will help me achieve my goals in the financial independence business while staying true to my visions and dreams.

I started to learn about leaders such as Bill Gates, Nelson Mandela, Gandhi, Martin Luther King Jr., Abraham Lincoln, Benjamin Franklin, Oprah Winfrey, Deepak Chopra, John C. Maxwell, Malcolm X, Elon Musk, Mother Teresa, and others.

I learned from each of them.

I found out the attributes and the things I liked about each one and considered who I wanted to become as a person. It was uplifting, and I realized how much growth I need. I took things from each person and will work to implement those attributes within myself.

From Nelson Mandela, I saw that he felt equal to all races. He had dignity and self-respect and demanded it. He did what it took to help his people, becoming militant at one point. He was loyal to the ladies he was with.

Deepak understands the power of mindfulness. He throws retreats, is knowledgeable and enlightened, stands in public and preaches his beliefs, and always has something to say.

Gandhi led with nonviolence, was well-read, spoke up for his people and his beliefs, stood in the face of danger, and led peacefully, even when violence was expressed on his people.

Martin Luther King studied Gandhi, led peacefully, and was a well-educated, powerful speaker who was not emotionally swayed. And most of all, he led people with love, like someone from our industry, and that's why I love this organization.

Malcolm X reformed himself.

Elon Musk believes in sustainable energy and is always working on that. He's an entrepreneur and goes all in. He is helping the planet go green.

Abraham Lincoln kept fighting even through his losses. Benjamin Franklin accumulated wealth and gave his ideas and inventions away for free to serve the people. He loved women.

John C. Maxwell teaches principles of success and strong leadership and loves to add value to others. He develops other leaders, helping leaders all over the world to increase their leadership abilities.

Oprah Winfrey has style and grace and is a generous public figure who overcame many challenges. She is a billionaire who likes money and uses it as a tool and is into mindfulness.

Bill Gates created a foundation for schools, lives luxuriously, and is a wealthy, innovative, business-savvy, edgy, and engaged learner. He is a good businessman. He is fair and warns others to protect their inventions.

All these people stood for their beliefs and their visions, even while having families. While building BMS, I feared I was being double-minded and preventing my financial independence business from flourishing. I realized that God gave me the time and income to have these dreams and visions come true and that everything was all part of one vision.

One thing I do to ensure that I don't do extra work and neglect the financial independence business is I dedicate my weekends and weekdays after four or five in the afternoon to that exclusively. I am determined to have my vision come true. I feel it is important to follow through, especially on this book, because this is a big tool in the world peace movement, including the movie and the nonprofit.

As I keep stretching myself and my mind for these goals, I see the vision becoming clearer. I am happy to be living with commitment and follow through, developing the character I want. I realized how important growing my leadership is. I started reading more and listening to more audios, picking up my personal development habits, and leading my team with more integrity. I see where I am struggling.

I was trying my hardest to learn how I could best help and serve the team. I realized that I had to lead by example. I always knew that, but it started to take on a new meaning. I had to start cleaning up my life, examining my routines, seeing where I was following through and not. I wanted to reevaluate and see how I am taking care of my mental, emotional, spiritual, and physical being.

After reading a personal development book, I realized how much I needed to get back into meditation, which I believe takes care of everything. Deep breathing is a workout for the body. It connects me with infinite wisdom, and God's compassion and grace heal me mentally and emotionally. I was getting bogged down and not following through on things I was committed to in my own life. I needed to free myself from being at Pop's house so much. I realized I could still help him from a distance. It at least helped to have the option to do so. I do have the funds, but the income does help.

I know he will lose his aide service when they see drugs around the house. If I leave him, these gangsters will take over the house, and a lot of other things that I want to avoid will happen. I go there facing his bad company and his drug habits, but he's my father. I said that if I'm going to help the world, I should be able to help my father. If I cannot help him and Trisha, as his son, my sister and I will have to move him from that location.

Another major lesson is that I cannot let my emotions get the best of me.

For example, I said hello to a neighbor, and for no reason, he cursed me.

If I did let my emotions control me, I would not be writing this. The mental abuse from my father had taken a toll on me emotionally, preventing me from thinking straight and doing my work. I would want to run home and take a nap, just to recuperate.

That's when I realized how valuable and important planning the day was so that when I have emotional experiences, I could still follow through with my goals. When I do follow through, the emotions evaporate into thin air.

I'm becoming more disciplined to where my emotions don't rule me, and my schedule is setting me up for success in both businesses and my personal life. This allows me to stay out more instead of running home into my comfort zone. They say the shark grows according to the size of the tank.

I want my tank to be the world.

I am currently and constantly fighting the habits of mediocrity and comfortability with discipline and following through. As I started journaling and meditating and getting more focused, it led to better schedules and more reflection and evaluation of myself. In my journal, I write about my lessons and highlights. I'm growing a great deal and learning to appreciate others so much more.

Continuing on the growth journey, how will I get stronger?

The growth has been happening in a few areas: my work ethic, receiving mentorship, being a mentor, and heightening awareness of the things I will study, how I will move forward, determining what my discipline will look like, and the way the world peace movement will manifest.

How will everything grow?

I had a serious surge of clarity and positive energy take over me over the past twenty-four hours. Yesterday, I started working on some things after Christmas brunch was over. Brunch lasted from noon until about five. Before leaving to go to brunch, I got what was probably the most sleep I have had all year, even though I left the light on and didn't even get under the sheets.

I gave from the heart. I'm not sure how well received my gifts to my mom and my big sister were. Well, my mom and sister both put up their clocks. My mom laughed when I gave it to her.

I sent out over two hundred texts and connected with a few hundred people, a soft touch. Then instead of going home, I went to a cafe, and I worked on pulling out the best qualities from the ten people I researched in the past month and created a list of qualities I would want.

I wrote about it all from memory because it was significant to me. I studied them intentionally. I want to become the best leader I could be. So I studied great leaders. I also studied my calendar intensely, and after examining things I would need to do weekly, I realized I could do it all. But it will take precision and follow through to grow Body, Mind, and Soul, work on this book, build my financial independence business, and make time for both my group and myself.

The biggest challenge would be following through and not getting distracted by my emotions. I need to make sure I am well prepared. When I say prepared, I mean having food, necessities, liquids, and maintaining energy levels.

When I say making time for myself, after reflecting on the past year, I saw how important certain routines are. Waking up at a scheduled time, journaling, and making time for reflection and evaluation all helps keep me focused on achieving my wins.

The next thing is my spirituality. The more I'm connected with my higher self, the better my life gets. This is the main priority. Keeping my health up is very important as well. I made time to grow in all areas so I can learn how to get everything done: build BMS, cultivate the world peace movement, and handle all the necessary studying, and develop my book. Most of all, I focused on growing my leadership expertise to build my financial independence business.

Meditation is key and is vital to my success.

THE VISION

How do I plan on helping the world and creating world peace?

I will work externally and internally.

I want to help people cultivate their inner peace and work on their own energy and internal needs.

I could do that through BMS by approaching corporations, schools, government officials, major organizations, and homes to show them how to focus on the good and how to practice gratitude, mindfulness and cultivate compassion. I could show them how to cultivate those attributes through tools used in daily activities, even in the workplace. Employers should be happy to do so because they and their employees will become more profitable to their jobs, their job performance and efficiency will increase, and more revenue will be generated due to them working on themselves internally. Period.

Next, we're going to work on external systems. The world is in pretty good shape, but we're destroying it rapidly.

We have to reduce fossil fuel use, carbon emissions, and many nonessential destructive materials.

We need to stop producing so many animals. Agriculture and cultivating fresh produce are necessary and can take over many animal farms.

In impoverished areas throughout the world, we should start producing more agriculture, empowering communities, and helping to clean up carbon emissions. We need this wherever people are impoverished. We should make numerous implementations in this way, placing them in homes, balconies, and park areas. Some countries are even doing hydroponics underground.

The next thing to consider is how we convert and reduce other greenhouse gas emissions. Next would be examining how we use cars. Thank God Elon Musk learned how to innovate and utilize solar cars. We have to jump on and expand upon that.

We have to create more efficient cities and communities. Elon Musk would be a genius to head that project. He has methods on how to distribute power to all of the United States, all from two plots of land: one hundred square miles for solar panels and a one-square-mile area for batteries. He has the technology in store for us to generate solar energy using generators, windmills, and whatever it takes.

Then we need to work on other energy sources and reboot the whole system. We can utilize existing electric companies and related industries into helping with this transition to solar energy, helping them gain skills in a new field within the new industry, making sure we don't put people out on the streets. We can think ahead to set up severance packages and help with job placement in the new and upcoming systems.

When we go help impoverished areas, leaders of their governments are going to get involved. We would need someone like John Maxwell or even his organizations to teach the political leaders how to be leaders and not take from their people. I know in Trinidad, Jamaica, Guyana, and other places, there are leaders who take more than they help. Those locations are close to my heart and my mind because of my business partners, fiancée, and my family. There are other places like Venezuela, Haiti, Columbia, African countries, and places in America and all over the whole world who need to learn those leadership skills.

Many governments take the majority of resources for themselves and don't spread them to the people, their people, the people they are in office to serve. They take what they want for themselves. That's another reason people do not like politicians. We must make sure wealth is distributed at a somewhat moderate rate, where people can eat and live more affordably. Let's implement tools to help produce agriculture more abundantly, making healthy food more accessible and not so expensive.

Reducing meat consumption will reduce the demand and supply. People will eat better because they will consume less hormone-produced and fatty foods and will have access to more fresh produce. Meat consumption is literally destroying the planet, externally and internally.

Think about it: the related carbon emissions are destroying the ozone layer. The drugs that are injected into these animals to make them bigger and to produce more meat and offspring are giving us diseases such as diabetes, high cholesterol, heart attacks, and unnecessary fat deposits. Then the pharmaceutical companies give us humans drugs for the diseases caused by the production of our food and meats, which is, again, a double whammy on both sides. I know these are controversial topics.

We can easily work with the same meat providers, and they can learn how to produce nonmeat or vegan products.

Pharmaceutical companies and meat producers do not have to lose power or money. They could work throughout the transition. They can find better ways to produce nutritious vegetation. The farmers and meat producers can learn to make fun vegetarian and vegan products.

Ford didn't want to transition away from his model for the first car, right? People didn't even want cars. They couldn't think past a horse. He lost a lot of money for not wanting to produce a second model.

There are many times we don't want to shift as people, but it's necessary to do so. It is very much necessary in a lot of areas.

I feel sexism is dying down, but we have to make sure women have their rights and have a voice and that their viewpoints are taken into consideration.

I don't believe religious beliefs should segregate us. I feel there should be one thing everyone knows: every religion has beauty in it. No religion calls for war. We should highlight the beauty in all religions and respect each one because each religion says that we are not supposed to be judging others.

That's for God to do. God is the judge. So why do we feel we can judge others? If our religions are telling us not to judge others, we should stop telling people one way is the right and only way. Love people for who they are and allow them to have their own beliefs.

In every religion, God is full of grace, love, and understanding. People think they know what is right and wrong, and they are strong in their own beliefs that their way is better. Comparing and judging creates that segregation, inferiority and superiority complexes. We need to unite and love one another and respect each other for their differences.

I respect people for their beliefs and embrace everyone with joy and love.

We shouldn't cast our beliefs on others, viewing our choices as the only way, because that creates segregation.

We have to reduce the inferiority and superiority complexes, and that is not just for religions. That is with police officers and civilians, with teachers and students, parents and children, the government and the common man (person), and the wealthy and the poor.

Most wealthy people are wealthy because they worked for it. I'm not saying people with less wealth do not work. We all make different decisions on how to create income based on our knowledge, needs, wants, desires, and most of all, our associations. Some children reap the benefits through inheritance but not in most cases.

The government officials are supposed to be there to serve the common man. The common man should be happy and feel blessed when he gets to see a government official. Government officials should be working to provide the best possible lifestyle for their citizens.

We need to teach the right type of leadership. If people are not willing to change and are living in the old ways, then they should either be removed or educated.

That goes for police officers, teachers, and parents. We have to remember that we were once young people. We have to be careful how we speak to people and treat one another.

I think some officers are not confident in their level of battle because some are gaining weight and remain unknowledgeable on defense and how to protect themselves, so they lash out in fear. They act like the number-one gang.

They have to work on those things and work on creating that tranquility within themselves.

We have to sign a world treaty with everybody. We will come back to this.

Let's go back.

We have parents, but how do they treat their children? They should be educated on how to treat their children, with the topics from Body, Mind, and Soul and other great organizations. This education has to be put on television. These things have to be broadcasted and must become mainstream. These things are rooted in common sense but are forgotten because they are not repeated or practiced. These ideas are not expanded upon or shared with the world, unlike the Kardashians or *MTV Cribs* or whatever you want to say that's high in society right now.

We have to teach morals and principles again. We have to teach people how to love, motivate, coach, and nurture one another. That goes for teachers and parents working with kids too. Parents, teachers, and schools must work as one on this. This also includes executives, employers, employees, and our model of democracy as a whole. All organizations need to have lessons on how to grow in their humanity and how to grow in peace, unity, compassion, and love.

We've got to understand that technology is expanding. We have to make room for that.

Technology will take over many jobs. With fewer jobs, we will have to create credits or a point system for people, something like the unemployment or the Social Security system.

How do you get credits? Everybody will get a standard credit and can earn more through creative and innovative work and care-related work.

In impoverished areas, we will implement systems and aid them with resources to help them thrive.

We will work to make clean water systems because everybody should have clean water. Solar energy should be the predominant source of energy. Energy should be provided throughout the world. We have to transition to solar energy. We must implement energy in all places that don't have energy sources.

Everyone should have homes. We can use 3D printing, which is very cost-efficient.

We start by tracking down the most marginalized, underserved locations and work on them. Then we work on our neighborhoods and our homes and clean up both the shelter system and jails, making them emulate those in Sweden and countries with humane, fruitful jail systems. That's how jail should be. We have to stop treating prisoners like caged animals and help them reform themselves to reenter society.

Love and proper education can heal people.

I was an EMT for four years, and homeless people do not like to go to homeless shelters.

My father did not want to enter a homeless shelter, and I did not want to leave him there. The people working there were not helpful. They are doing a job and have to protect themselves. All love and peace to them.

But it's not about that. It is an unsafe environment. People feel they'll get robbed and beat up. Shelter systems have to become reform systems as well. These shelters should be clean and well kept. If machines are not cleaning the facilities, you must have the necessary people who should get paid well for their work.

We will have to work incrementally. To have things work, we are going to need creative strategies delegated out with precision and care.

Everywhere throughout the world is implementing meditative practices, maintaining and growing health in the mental, spiritual, emotional, and physical areas of everyone. More vegetarian and vegan diets are being implemented. There are studies that show yoga and meditation reduce stress, which reduces cancer because the genes are already in you. Cancer cells get activated by stress, and stress is the leading factor of disease and sickness. We have to help people reduce stress. It can consist of different exercises, meditative practices, and different food choices. Meditation does not have to be limited to deep breathing. There are chanting, prayer, exercise, gratitude, art, journaling, and many more options.

It can be physical movement as well, but be careful, as some exercises may stress the body too much and can cause more harm than good. Meat, when not cultivated appropriately, also puts stress on the body. I'm not saying not to eat meat because of my love or sacred view of animals. I'm not saying that I'm some holy guy. I'm merely saying it is destroying the planet. If we care about our kids and the future, what are we doing?

What are we going to do?

If you do not care, say you do not care. Period. If you do, work toward changing certain habits for society's benefit. Our habits can be overcome and must be for the sake of future generations.

We have to decide to move forward in a positive direction.

As we are changing leaders, correcting systems, and working on unity, we can go places that are in conflict and work to arrange a sit-down with those in charge, even if we have to infiltrate their systems and do nontraditional things in order to secure that sit-down.

We sit down and figure out how we can come to peace mutually, leading to a world peace treaty. This world should not have war. I love Martin Luther King for saying, "Hate cannot drive out hate; only love can do that."

That is how many great leaders lead.

We need to create equality. We need to work on treating each other with respect, integrity, and love. If we treat everybody with respect and love and have integrity in our actions, this world would be a better place.

This world would be healed. We would not even need police or a court system.

We have to transition our leaders to lead in a way that adds value to the people.

We have to clean up all organizations and implement meditative and physical practices like yoga and other fun stress-reduction activities into society.

The reason I suggest yoga is because almost anyone can do it, and it does not require many resources. It's very hard to get hurt unless you try to make more advanced moves before you're ready. It maintains your body and connects you with your mind. Meditation also helps you calm your thoughts, which, when overwhelming, can create stress. We should be teaching positive affirmations and gratitude and using uplifting books, prayers of whatever religion, exercises, dance, and whatever is fun, in more spaces.

We can have a fun world with joy and laughter.

We can do all of it by removing the nonsense and negativity.

We have to transition in this direction.

THE PLAN

First, I'm going to continue building my financial independence business because charity starts at home. If I'm going to go out and help the world, I have to help my family. I'm going to make sure everybody's secure and that we are well-off. This will allow me to focus on the bigger picture and implement all these different pieces.

I started that business for the money, but then I saw the impact it had on people and how much we helped people with life. I realized the kind of leader that this was pushing me to become. My mentor helped me grow in many aspects of maturity and leadership. From there, I decided I need to stay active within the industry to become a better leader to help the world. I understand we are going to work in life. I'm going to work toward what I want. World peace is a big goal of mine. My fiancée and I talked about this before we decided to even go out seriously.

While growing my financial independence business, I will develop my connections with people who can and are willing to serve the idea and project and wealthy people who put their money into charity. With God's blessings, the charity will be the nonprofit for the world peace project. This book is going to show how we can heal the planet.

This is going to go viral and become a movie that will be action-packed, fun, down-to-earth, heartwarming, inspiring, and motivational, with a lot of life lessons. We are going to highlight certain stories and show how we could clean up society. We will show the connections being made, the growth that we had to go through, and how the plans will come to fruition, from the development of the organizations to the making of the movie. It will include the struggles and all the overcoming.

As we increase our assets by growing the financial independence business and maintaining Body, Mind, and Soul, I will have income there as well. I will transition from taking care of my father to being able to hire an aide to take care of him. I have to change his situation. It will be by changing his location or insisting that, unless both he and Trisha attend Narcotics Anonymous to heal themselves, I would have to kick Trisha out. Either way, the gangsters will come back if my pops is left by himself.

He will end up letting them in if he feels lonely. Yes, he has to make the decision for himself, but his environment is very important. I feel my sister and I will have to choose what his environment will be, unless he and Trisha make the right decisions.

I'll transition and free up my time to focus on my financial independence business. Body, Mind, and Soul will be implemented within major corporations. Body, Mind, and Soul will eventually go global and become a nonprofit somewhere down the path. As I learn how to create the nonprofit, I also plan on hiring a CEO and board members to build and run the project.

As I go through this, I will always study something. I will oversee things. I'm going to work with facilities and organizations that provide solar energy, agriculture, healthcare, health, and wellness treatments and work on shifting society toward more holistic healthcare. I will find and work with facilities that build homes, provide education, and clean water. I'm not here to recreate everything. I'm here to join us together as one and be a facilitator.

I don't want those organizations to be robbing people either. I will make sure the numbers are running right and that the workers and the communities are happy. The money we receive is going to the resources that we say we're going to provide and collaborating with amazing organizations.

We could connect with Doctors Without Borders, the Mother Teresa Foundation, John C. Maxwell and his EQUIP group, Bill Gates Foundation, Feed America, and many other great foundations out there.

We will transition appropriately into healing the earth instead of allowing it to continue on a path of destruction and chaos.

We'll be healing the planet internally and externally.

We'll find the right tactics and the right forces to work on the world peace treaty.

We will infiltrate the right systems and spaces to talk to the leaders to make sure we come to an understanding and appease and collaborate with all necessary parties with the ultimate goal of world peace.

We want all of society to be happy and content with understanding, compassion, and love.

Education systems will be changed, and the message of Body, Mind, and Soul will be amplified. Healthcare will be transformed since we'll be healing people through more preventative methods and better nourishment. There will be less medicine necessary. Society will become more holistic.

For the water system, the solar energy system proposed by Elon Musk, agriculture systems, and constructing homes from 3D printing, people in those industries will come to us. We will not even have to look for them because they'll hear about what we're doing, and we'll be able to collaborate with the best of the best. We'll have them all write proposals to show us what they can provide and how they can provide it. We will know all of the locations that need to be healed and supported.

That is what the board members of the world-peace-treaty movement will be doing. We will be facilitators and work with key people in creating what we need and getting the work done.

I will keep my cup full and fill myself up with joy and happiness so I can spread that all around the world. I will make sure my wife and family have a great life. We will travel and enjoy the luxuries of life, always making sure we give more than we take.

I will go overseas and make sure everything is working well. I'm not scared to fly into these places we're working on establishing often or periodically, whichever is necessary to make sure things are running smoothly. I will find honest, respectful people that believe in this vision, and we will make it happen together.

THE WORK

I got out early from work because the laundry was closed, and I could not do much for Pops. I made him food, cleaned some things, set up his clothes, and left. I listened to an audio and thought about my last chapter as I drove to Queens. I took a nap and meditated in the car. Today is January 1, 2020, a new decade.

The night before, I left my girl's house at 11:22 p.m., right before the ball drop. Her brother wanted to leave to get home and get some rest, and so did I.

My mom and I left in separate cars. I called my girl after my meditation. I meditated my way into the new year. I sat upright in meditation from 11:57 p.m. to 12:10 a.m., and I had a lot of good realizations. When I called her, she was upset and started crying. She said she wanted to bring the new year in together. I told her that I didn't know it was so important and that I loved her. I wanted to focus on myself.

Her mom, her dad, and her brother were talking about how good of a dancer she was and telling me I wouldn't be able to keep up with her for our wedding dance. My attitude was, "I'm a winner. I can do anything."

It is habitual for her mom to put things and people down. When you speak up and coach people, they listen. They're good people. I love them. I didn't want to bring the new year in with them for those reasons. Her brother said he was leaving, so it worked out. My mom and I left. Veni did not ask me to stay. They had me compare myself to Veni again. To me, I have many accomplishments that are incomparable. Some people are better at certain things. Anyone can learn whatever they want. I comforted her mind and let her know I loved her.

She was going to hot yoga, and I would have loved to go with her, but one thing I realized coming into a new year is not to get distracted by anyone and do the work I need to. They will learn how to cope and do their own things, and I will still make time for them on my time and would want them to do the same with me. This is going to be one of the greatest years of my life. We will achieve so much in our financial independence business. The biggest thing I learned is to pick up my phone.

I have a solid foundation and skill set. I will continue to stay consistent in my core habits and grow in the areas I need to. The biggest thing I learned in the last few months was that I cannot grow my people. Yes, I can add value, motivate them, and encourage them. The biggest thing I need to do is grow myself and lead by example.

How can I grow myself?

By following through on things, I say I will do. In the new year, I heard a lot of subtle hints from the universe to focus on my health. I will continue to get fit. The biggest thing I know I need is meditation. It helps build my confidence, compassion, focus, belief, and follow-through most of all. It allows me to be calm to serve others and not get anxious or act weird because I am nervous. Getting fit opens the door for me to serve people with nutritional therapy, personal training, and meditation. It is another way to transition my income. I have so many ways to make money.

This business is very spiritual. In school and work, you can just go in and do the work, and you can pass. Here, I feel God or the universe watches everything. I need to stay true to myself in all areas of my life, which I will.

I have to be committed to myself mentally, spiritually, emotionally, and physically. I'm not saying I have to be perfect, but I have to stay true to my priorities in those areas. God has love and grace and is the most merciful. I need to keep strong with my word, follow through in my life, and keep doing the work. Our organization says, "God, family, then business."

To us, people have three priority levels. My first priority is my future wife and kids and me. On the second level are our parents, three generations above and below, and our mentors and mentees.

Last, our siblings, extended family, friends, and acquaintances are the third priority. I think it makes perfect sense. I don't have a wife or kids yet. My focus is on me. This is the time to build a future for my kids and wife, which are coming soon. I realized how I need to build this business, enhance my leadership, leading myself because I need to be an example. I need to follow through on my schedule daily, weekly, monthly, and yearly while keeping and growing communication and connection with my team and family.

Building a better future also requires focusing on building new connections with all the people I work with. I have to make their lives better. I get to encourage people to live their best lives and clean up their finances and relationships, which will allow them to upgrade in their luxuries and options of life. My goal is to help people build their best life. They will be able to build their businesses and do anything they want.

Why am I qualified to lead others?

We can all grow to become leaders if we decide to develop in an area where we have knowledge to help others.

My expertise is in living life in the best way, with high morals and ethics, growing in all areas of mental, emotional, physical, and spiritual wellness. I'm qualified because I have written my first book, which is on self-help. The book is based on successful and scientific principles. I'm a certified integrative wellness and life coach and a nutritional therapist. I have worked with monks for four years, worked as an EMT, was a personal trainer, and graduated as a biochemist.

Most of all, I learned from successful, wealthy people who have great lives and great relationships, people with great results in all areas of their lives. They have great family relationships with their partners and kids. They are financially and physically up to par or better, and they do great charity work. I read, listen, and associate with these successful husbands, wives, pastors, business people, and many more.

I learned success principles in all areas of life. I teach by principle since I'm not perfect. If I am better off in certain areas or have knowledge, I can teach by real-life example. Within this year, I will sponsor twenty-plus people in width, meaning twenty direct mentees doing all that they agreed to for partnership. I will help them grow significantly, using the tools that I have learned from my direct mentor and from all the other successful people we have in our lives. I will be dedicating my nights and weekends to serving and building my team. My personal growth will remain high, and I will progress as needed to serve my team, so my team can use me as a resource to help develop their businesses.

I'm going to communicate and become the number one communicator I can be so I can get my foundation done.

One thing I learned in my business is that I get excited after I sponsor a few people. I want to see how I can serve them on an ongoing basis. I need to keep my momentum up in continuing to sponsor more awesome people and serve them by respecting the times we agree upon and by being considerate of them. The phases are going to be a great help. It helps keep people on track and build our leadership skills.

Anytime I'm doing something new, I will text Josiah for feedback, especially in the business. Thankfully, he created those systems. He said, "Jay, let me help you build this." He relates to and respects my mindset. Blessings come in ways you would often never expect.

I will finish this book, continue making calls for Body, Mind, and Soul, and do other work necessary such as videos, which I will continue to improve on. After the book is completed, I will study other topics, spending time weekly, for one to four hours, on different necessary topics to make the world peace project happen. This involves stuff like promoting and marketing the book, getting a literary agent, creating a nonprofit for both BMS and the world peace project, creating a screenplay and movie, and building connections with the people I need to help this vision happen. I need to learn how to create a board for both the world peace project and for BMS.

I will be working on these things as I maintain my meditation and physical activity, such as yoga, calisthenics, and weight training or martial arts. Other priorities include finding my first apartment and getting married, which will include learning to perform our dance and becoming looser within myself. I will create a greater bond with Veni, and we will be an inspiration to our families, our team, and the world.

We will learn to work together in all areas of life, being able to grow together spiritually, physically, mentally, and emotionally. Our parents won't have the same influence on us since we will be out of their homes. We will learn how to grow our businesses and our dreams together, becoming a unit, yet free enough to be ourselves individually.

This is how I see my future going within the next year or two. This is not fantasy. I will work with God and the universe to put in the work to manifest these things. I just read a devotional post from my fiancée:

"Not only do you have the responsibility toward your fellow human beings, but it is also your privilege to bring blessings and joy to your friends, family, and all those around you and to make a difference in the lives of as many people as possible. Lord, thank you that you have created this wonderful universe for us to enjoy in relationship with you. Help me this year to fulfill this potential. I have to make a difference in other people's lives."

I live this way, especially in the past two months, due to my mentor saying we should write down our goals daily. It also highlights a big lesson I learned from John C. Maxwell's *The 21 Irrefutable Laws of Leadership*: the law of the lid, which states that your leadership ability determines your level of effectiveness. I realized my capacity grew as I saw and was more connected with all the people I think of and will help.

I have observed that many people are focused on their well-being only. I'm not saying they do not care about others, yet they are not making it their responsibility to make an impact to affect and contribute to all those lives.

If you focus on your bills, your lifestyle, your goals, and your issues, the most you can hit is that level. Say that level is a five, the highest you can go is a four. You cannot achieve more because that's your lid. My lid has grown, and that is why I'm experiencing more energy, more determination, and more follow-through. I took my eyes off myself. Now, I'm focused on creating a life for my future wife, which begins in September, as well as for my future kids and our parents. Of course, this means being able to financially support them and growing our business to impact many other people's lives in a positive way and ultimately working to serve the world.

Sometimes it is hard to believe. I can achieve all that God has shown me, but only if I do the work, follow through, and live with urgency, strength, and compassion. I see it as possible and doable. It is happening. I have to keep going. I don't know where my lid is anymore, and when I do find it, I'll make sure it is high enough to fill more than only my goals and dreams.

I can continue to serve so many others. My mentor and the world have planted so many seeds in me over the last few years, especially from being surrounded by the positivity of our personal growth community and the profound and positive things my mentor has brought into my life. Another major lesson is to keep my head down and get the work done.

I see our New York team growing to theaters and getting much bigger this year. My relationships, bonds, and influence will grow massively within the team, pushing them forward. Working with Josiah and the team, we help our whole New York community grow and have functions sooner than we imagined. BMS grows through great marketing, advertising, and service, which extends by word of mouth as well, allowing us to create six figures of income this year, extend to corporations, and find the right people and help bring it all together.

We will receive great grants from the government to be able to serve even more schools before extending into more holistic services. BMS already includes nutritional therapy, life and health coaching, health and wellness instructors, and cosmetology. Eventually, we will extend to massage therapists, oil specialists, acupuncturists, chiropractors, and other ideas, plus medicine for things that are necessary. We will work with a team with the vision and expertise to help us create health and wellness centers throughout the world within the next decade, especially in major areas where we are implementing the world peace project to serve those communities.

These big wellness centers and training for staff will change the wellness industry dramatically, helping heal people with nutrition and relieving stress through methods such as yoga, meditation, and whatever else the holistic world sees fit. Stress and bad food activate the genes for sicknesses, so we will teach people how to heal themselves. These programs will be offered for all first responders and in corporations, police stations, hospitals, schools, activity centers, all organizations, and homes.

Remember, world peace starts with you. We need to heal our own energies, for that is what spreads. My friend and I were having a talk about this yesterday. I shared with him an example of Veni and I arguing in the car one day.

In the car next to us, the same thing was happening. They were yelling. We related that to him being sick and how his sister got sick soon after.

I should have recommended that he get checked up. The real thing that I'm getting at is that our energy spreads.

That's why I meditate. Remember, meditation could be prayer, chanting, and deep breathing, which I think is the best for healing and anchoring because it takes a strong focus to harness our energy, clean it, and purify it. Practicing being a good person is a great meditation as well. That's why I love my financial independence business because it helps teach people great success principles and, in general, how to be a good person.

Our energies affect everything. We should be taught how to heal ourselves in all industries. This will be a major step toward world peace. This book will be endorsed by major influencers. All these visions can and will be executed. This will come into fruition. I feel it in my gut. The book will be endorsed by strong key leaders within months of its release and then move on to the bestseller list before production of the movie begins.

The world will manifest this project for the greater good. While the book circulates and the production of the movie continues, I will update the first book to make it more reputable. As I grow this year, I will develop in all fields. I previously mentioned some of them: marketing, advertising, creating a nonprofit, producing a screenplay and movie, and cultivating an amazing board of directors for these organizations, and more. The world peace project will do so many amazing things.

Solar energy will be massively implemented throughout the world. There may be companies that will lose compensation due to these system changes and less demand for their supply. They will have the option to buy in and support the movement or just receive credits to make the transition easier on them, like a severance package. I think Elon Musk's mind would be a great asset and that he has drastically changed the world for the better. I am a big fan of his work so far.

I see systems being implemented in the most impoverished areas throughout the world and beyond. This covers all continents, transforming places, starting with the most impoverished to the most lavish. To do this, we will need strong leadership and strong leadership development. I feel John C. Maxwell will be a great asset in this area because he has transformed many lives and organizations, including mine. He can help us, wake up. He can help us work with all the governments throughout the world, teaching leaders to help their people and serve them. We can work with top professionals in finance industries to help generate profit statements so members of governments and industries will be compensated appropriately during the transition. They can compile the numbers to make the transition smoother and show these organizations how the numbers will project. These operations will be going on simultaneously yet with smooth execution because of well-thought-out applications and implementation. That will be completed as the movie is produced.

Next is vegetation. Agriculture and vegetation production should be expanded throughout the world, especially in areas considered to be a nuisance so everyone everywhere can be a contribution to healing the planet.

We should learn from industries that have the technology and pull from other great industries to produce organic agriculture on farms throughout the world. In the new farms we create, just like in the business, the agriculture systems could fit in the smallest homes and be big enough to span fields and stadiums. We can make that accessible to all of society since certain industries have already mastered the science and distribution.

Communities will be able to distribute affordable produce in supermarkets, at any level seen fit, and they could even produce and distribute their own company goods. A big mission is to heal our ozone and rid the planet of carbon emissions. What would aid that?

Of course, I think it is necessary to stop and destroy mass meat consumption. Many markets and industries will transition, such as some pharmaceutical companies, medical centers, and farms producing meat. We will still need medication but only for things only medicine can help with: birth pain, surgeries, and other trauma and medical issues. All these markets will have a way to transition and will be aided in the process to move toward world peace. We will support them on the conversion to relieve the chaos.

The pharmaceutical companies can use their energy, knowledge, and resources to produce vitamins and supplements and become an asset. Medical centers can combine with wellness centers. We will still need doctors for surgery, pediatricians, birth, and so forth. Everything else can be treated through holistic practices, which can take over traditional medical schools and medical centers and help these companies change and facilitate these ideas. Converting animal farms to producing nonanimal products and directing meat makers to making tasty nonmeat options may sound drastic, but it's necessary.

Do you really care about our future generations and the planet? We need to make deadlines and transitional goals to help implement this all. We have limited time before we reach a point where destruction of this planet is irreversible.

I know the government can slow down actions; therefore, we need to all be on the same page and show how smooth the transformations can go. Once we establish what can go wrong, we can plan the preventative measures to have in place to make this movement successful.

We need to move on this.

We can work with influencers or successful entrepreneurs like Oprah, Jay-Z, and Will Smith, and motivational speakers, actors, major business owners like Gates, Bezos, and many other leaders to have this happen efficiently and effectively. Among them are people like Deepak Chopra, the Dalai Lama, and other major leaders that will help us implement the right practices and teachings for the upcoming holistic health and wellness centers.

We need someone or a group to be at the forefront. John C. Maxwell can help us get into the government and leadership training in all industries, and Elon Musk can help implement solar energy everywhere. Strong leading industries in the appropriate fields can help cultivate agriculture and identify people to lead the developments by collaborating with facilities already in place and helping unify opposing forces, working with them all to be a resource.

All throughout the world, the wellness movement is key because it will help us open up the minds of everyone as the transition happens. Mindfulness helps with change and adaptation. We can help people take their eyes off themselves and remember that we are all one. The planet is like our body, and we humans are representative of cells, all working together. We all make the world function and come together.

One side of the movement includes working on the internal healing of all major organizations, including first responders, teachers, corporations, governments, and more.

Working externally, we will implement systems to heal places and communities. That entails solar energy, agriculture, wellness, leadership, and building homes and other items through 3D printing.

Why am I going on this path I have chosen?

One of the main reasons I build the financial business is to first grow as a leader.

Second, charity starts at home. My financial independence will support my family and allow me to focus more energy on the world peace project.

Also, the book, the movie, BMS, and the financial independence business will help me make many connections, and they will all want to contribute to the cause.

This movement is not for me; it is for the world.

I am doing this because this is what God, the universe, and the world have nurtured me to be. My mom was always giving and caring. My father is a happy-go-lucky, risk-taking guy. There were so many other reasons why.

I strongly believe that the world will support this movement. The book and movie will create a connection with the entertainment industry. BMS will connect with all major organizations. We can work with all other major industries in the field, healing people internally and opening their minds by working with some of the biggest influencers in order to build and implement these systems.

Some of the biggest influencers, such as the Dalai Lama, Oprah, Deepak, and other religious and spiritual leaders, can work together with us on this.

This will break segregation, and we will see the beauty in everyone's religion and culture.

The centers developed will cater to all religions and people coming together around common good practices. We will make sure to show discrimination faced and performed by various religions and people. Showing their healing and the beauty of them all in the movie.

The production of these things will draw the right leaders and create a board of directors to lead these endeavors. I envision leadership training led or developed by the biggest leadership guru of our time, John C. Maxwell, and his team, which would help us get into every country and support the healing of the planet, reminding everyone of their power. We are not trying to take over. We are not trying to monopolize. We are aiming to keep money in the people's pockets. The systems we create will heal the planet and give our future generations a chance.

Half of the money from the book and the movie's box office will go to the world peace organization.

We can do this. I love you.

Zoom back to me on the patio plugging into a global conference with the board of directors, calling in to make sure everything's on track.

"Hey, team, how are you guys?"

In the end, we sign the treaty of world peace.

Perfect. That's the end.